Living the spiritually authentic
& intimate life…

THE
INTIMATE
SOUL

Laura V. Hyde

THE INTIMATE SOUL
Laura V. Hyde

FIRST EDITION

Published by Sustainable Solutions Press
PO Box 607, Grand Haven, MI 49417

Manufactured in the United States of America
ISBN: 0-9658150-2-1

SUSTAINABLE SOLUTIONS PRESS

PUBLISHING STATEMENT
OF PURPOSE

We believe in the greatness of the human capacity when aligned with the integrity of one's higher will. While seeking to endorse the spirit of abundance, we encourage all to express themselves in giving ways, knowing we all succeed to the extent we share our gifts. We value the world as a place of healing and foster the exchange of knowledge which lovingly affirms our oneness.

Sustainable Solutions Press

THE INTIMATE SOUL may be ordered through:

Infinite Wisdom, PO Box 607, Grand Haven, MI, 49417, 888.732.2393, or by visiting Laura's website at: www.laurahyde.com, or through Amazon.com or barnesandnoble.com.

Bookstores please contact one of our distributors:

New Leaf Distributing Company

Partners Book Distributors

Ingram Books

Matters of the Heart—a free quarterly newsletter written by national author and speaker Laura V. Hyde that will inspire and empower you in every area of your life. To *receive Matters of the Heart* please call: 888.732.2393 or e-mail us at: laurahyde@novagate.com

Other books by Laura V. Hyde:

Gifts of the Soul

DEDICATION

This book stems from the culmination of numerous life events that have taken me closer to my own soul and toward a profoundly intimate and authentic relationship with God and those around me. This journey has allowed me to experience genuine love and joy, and in the true spirit of abundance, I dedicate this book to all of you who wish to experience the deepened intimacy and heartfelt love that you deserve.

Cover artwork/artist—©Stephanie Pui-Mun Law
Title: "Infinite Angels"

Stephanie: *"...I saw two people made of gold dancing the earth's dances. They turned so perfectly that together they were the axis of the earth's turning. They were light; they were molten, changing gold [...] Manes grew tall into feathers that shone -- became light rays...one of the dancers is always a man and the other a woman. The man and woman grow bigger and bigger. So bright, all light. They are tall angels in two rows. They have high white wings on their backs. Perhaps there are infinite angels..."*

(**For more information on Stephanie's artwork, please visit her website at: www.shadowscapes.com)

"Infinite Angels...Light-filled, synchronized, and joyous, this beautifully pivoting male and female "angel" symbolizes the balancing of the divine masculine and feminine aspects inherent within each of us. Capturing the essence of genuine intimacy, 'Infinite Angels' wonderfully illustrates the depth of magnificence and love within us, inspiring and inviting us to expose our deepest most glorious selves...."

LAURA

FOREWORD

As a publisher, I realize that most "forewords" are written by someone who is an expert in the field of a book's subject. Thus when asked by Laura to write the foreword for *The Intimate Soul*, I was hesitant at first because I questioned my own "expertise" in the field of relationship and intimacy. Yet, as I thought about it, I recalled the growth that I have experienced as a result of my relationship with Laura. The lessons have been as rewarding as they have been challenging and I am extremely honored to write the forward to this monumental book.

Within these pages, Laura boldly addresses this issue: if we were truly honest with ourselves, what we fear more than anything else is ...intimacy.

Unresolved intimacy issues cause our soul to ache. Getting in touch with these issues as Laura skillfully explains, is an internal process that "...can lead you to the doorway where your deepest most intimate self dwells; it's the magnetic energy compelling you toward truth, love and meaning; it's the gateway for connecting intimately with God, yourself and others."

Laura excels at expressing the compelling essence of a life lived authentically and intimately. She is one courageous woman. Laura dares to share her experiences with intimacy (and mine as well!) so that the rest of us can benefit. She is a master at combining her wisdom with practical guidance.

Never in this book is advice given that Laura has not actually lived. She is a walking, talking, living testimony to congruence. She writes with such truth that the words seem to leap right from the page and into your heart.

The Intimate Soul demonstrates how to align our actions and beliefs with the guidance of our highest intention. It's time to build upon the foundation of real internal honesty, and thereby, strengthen the bond of love so that one can compassionately create a safe place for his or her soul to grow.

So, to the reader, if you are going through life accompanied by a persistent internal ache, rest assured that the pain will go away. And, further, know that you possess all that is necessary, right now, to remove that pain forever. Laura has done it and is sharing with you how to access that splendor within so your life may be filled with genuine intimacy. All that is asked of you, is that you be truly willing to do the inner-work ("*in-to-me-see*").

And, to you, Laura, this book is a tribute, a celebration of your soulful insight and a testimony to your inspired courage to share what you have experienced so that this world is a better place to live. I salute you, Honey.

Tom Stevenson
November 28, 2000

TABLE OF CONTENTS

FILLING THE VOID

Even through the darkest phase
Be it thick or thin,
Always someone marches brave
Here beneath my skin.
Maybe a great magnet pulls
All souls towards truth,
Or maybe it is life itself
That feeds wisdom
To its youth.
Constant craving has always been....
k.d. lang, Cd *Ingenue*

*E*ach of us, at one time or another, must come face to face with our own personal "void," a place deep inside, like a dark cavern, where the uncertainty of who we are and why we're here resides. It's the cavity of emptiness that eats away at our happiness, inner peace, and self-esteem. It's similar to living in a dungeon, blocked from the light of our innermost self, where we feel alone and lonely with little hope of getting out. Like a hungry child, the void causes us to crave something, or someone, to fill us up. Yet nothing seems to make it go away, at least, not for very long. Eating, drinking, buying "things," having sex, exercising, working, or developing a new relationship does not do the trick—not even Prozac. The void is a steady gnawing, a hollowness we desperately attempt to fill with fleeting diversions. Sound familiar?

1

(If you're answer is, "No, I never feel that way," then perhaps it is time to be really honest with yourself and take a personal inventory of your life.)

I remember facing my own personal void in the early 90's. At that time, I referred to it as "the dark abyss" or "black hole" because that's how it felt. The void was not always noticeable. I could easily distract myself from it with a little relationship drama here, or a new project there. Yet as my healing continued and I became more aware of who I was and why I was here, the task of distracting myself became more challenging. It was as if my soul was saying, "It's going to take more to fill me up than just another relationship or project— I'm starving for something *REAL!*" And, of course, "real" meant something of substance, something of true meaning and depth, something that would genuinely connect me with my innermost self.

I was on an infinite loop...searching. Eventually, my search revealed that nothing outside of me was ever going to replenish the emptiness I was feeling. In fact, it was only taking me farther away from my soul. And as I looked around, I saw more of the same. Everywhere I turned it seemed someone was attempting to fill their own void with food, alcohol, sex, material items, work, relationship pursuits—the list of options was as endless as the number of people searching.

During this same time, I discovered a connection between the "something" I was longing for and what *A Course in Miracles* referred to as my "part" in God's Plan. Gradually, my craving began to transform from an incessant, barren hunt into a beautiful healing gift; it became the catalyst that moved me away from the futility of external seeking to the abundance of my own soul. The journey was a pathway of heartfelt intimacy: intimacy with God, others, and myself. It was the beginning of not only living an authentic and fulfilling life, but the beginning of life itself.

Any void you have ever felt, or will ever feel, can never be filled with anything outside yourself. There is not enough food, alcohol, money or accomplishments to take away the emptiness you feel deep within, simply because the seeking of those things actually take you *away* from your self. We are an addicted-oriented society. Escapism through addiction either leads to recovery or death. Our blackest moments often occur after we have been caught up in some outside diversion. Like a towering wall, the external activity blocks the light of our soul. In essence, we allow the wall of external activity to replace the face of God, and that becomes the source of our pain.

The only thing that will eliminate your void is genuine, heartfelt intimacy. True intimacy comes from connecting with, and knowing, your own soul, from experiencing and seeing the Face of God. For within your soul exists a wellspring of love, desire, passion and deep thirst for all that life has to offer, including all of the emotions that exist within our human experience.

In the midst of your void resides a hunger, a constant craving. This craving can lead you to the doorway where your deepest most intimate self dwells; it's the magnetic energy compelling you toward truth, love and meaning; it's the gateway for connecting intimately with God, yourself and others. Your craving is actually the desire that propels you inward. Once you realize there is nothing outside yourself that can satisfy your craving, and you declare, "I've had enough, there *must* be a better way," Spirit, ever willing to respond to your slightest invitation, will gently open the rooms containing your truth, strengths, ideas and inspiration.

Marianne Williamson once revealed, "We are deeply afraid of the silence, the void, the emptiness. The void is not material; it is force. The void is where God is. God is the potential fullness gushing out from every empty space, the ever-present possibility of a magic moment or miraculous thought."

A sense of wholeness will only come from looking within since all the love you ever need already exists inside you. What if right now, in this very moment, you began to accept that you already *have* and *are everything*?

Years ago, I saw this truth in action when I met a man diagnosed with multiple sclerosis. It was obvious this person had very little in the way of material things. In fact, he was confined to a wheel chair and had difficulty merely getting around. My first reaction was sympathy. Yet, as I saw him interact with others, I witnessed such joy and peace that I ceased thinking about his physical condition. His fulfillment came from something far beyond his five senses. He was a testimonial to love without conditions. He gave his love freely, and people reflected love back to him without reservation. Realizing there were no accidents, I knew this person was an integral part of my spiritual awakening, for his life was truly his message, and his message was authentic and intimate.

You don't have to go through life feeling empty, nor do you need to be afraid of the magnificence and love residing within you. It is our light we fear the most not our darkness, so facing the void is the beginning of experiencing profound intimacy.

Must we experience futile searching before we turn to God? Unfortunately, for most of us, it appears we must. Why? Because pain is such a powerful motivator for change. Think about the times in your life when you have been most willing to try something new. Usually, they have followed on the footsteps of a difficulty or crisis. The ego's motto is "seek but do not find." This vicious cycle of seeking keeps us spiraling downward in the endless search toward nothingness. And like one of my daughter's favorite movies—the mystical yet realistic *Never Ending Story*—what could possibly be more empty and depressing than existing in the land of nothing?

So, right now, ask yourself, "When do I feel the most empty?" "How do I try to fulfill myself?" "What do I turn to when I want to fill my void?" Answering these probes will take you deeper into yourself.

As you begin to learn about the void and notice how you respond to it, you will find that the void feels strongest when you're not aligned with your soul. Or another way to look at it, you will feel most incomplete when you are engaged in something that does not ring of truth to your authentic self. This often occurs upon the completion of some external pursuit. After the "high" has worn off, an automatic "low" will follow.

Unlike these inauthentic diversions, *genuine intimacy fills our void.* When we dig deeply into our selves and taste the fruits of our own soul, we are no longer hungry. True intimacy requires self-honesty and the willingness to delve within and face our fears. Allowing our emptiness to surface is the only way we will experience the light inside. By doing so, we discover that we don't need to be anymore "spiritual" than we already are; we need only be willing to be the authentic intimate souls we were born to be.

I have been inspired to write *The Intimate Soul* because I have experienced the void and the healing of it through genuine intimacy. And though I still have moments when I'm tempted to go back into the void, inevitably, I am beckoned by the compelling Voice for Love to choose differently. Having made the commitment to be a vehicle for healing and service, I share my deepest insights, thoughts, feelings and experiences with you throughout this book.

As you read *The Intimate Soul*, dare to expand your mind, open your heart and embrace your deepest self. Fears are bound to surface. Feelings of self-doubt will arise. Skepticism may rear its head. But then again, this book isn't for those looking for a quick, easy and soul-less approach. It's designed to empower you to release whatever is not authentically you, and that demands courage and willingness. Releasing your attachment to other people's opinions, letting go of outcome, having faith and trust in a higher power, practicing forgiveness, listening to your inner guidance—all of these qualities are not attained by walking the road most traveled. They are captured by those who desire to live a powerfully authentic and intimate life, by those willing to be true to who they are, no matter what others think, say or do. Living the spiritually authentic and intimate life is not for everyone, so the question becomes, "Is it for you?"

PRAYER for INTIMACY

Dear Mother/Father God, we desire to experience our spiritual, emotional and physical wholeness, to feel the depths of our own soul, to taste the sweet river of love flowing within us. Please help us call forth our most authentic and intimate selves and to drop whatever is not inherently us in the recognition that our fulfillment comes not from without, but from deep within where You reside...

...May all beings awaken to their inner-light and share the remembrance of their oneness; May all hearts rejoice in the joy of their inherent love-filled essence; May all souls remember that their purpose for living is to extend love in all that they think, say, and do.

INTIMACY WITH SELF & GOD

*From the beginning of my life, I have been looking
for Your face, but today, I have seen It.
Today I've seen the charm, the beauty, the
unfathomable grace of the face that I was looking
for, the day I found You.
And those who laughed and scorned me yesterday
are sorry that they were not looking as I did.
I am bewildered by the magnificence of Your beauty
and wish to see You with a hundred eyes.
My heart has burned with passion and has searched
forever for this wondrous beauty that I now behold.
I'm ashamed to call this love human and afraid of
God to call it divine...*

Jalaleddin Rumi,
13th century poet

STRIPPING AWAY THE MASK

The authentic self is the soul made visible.
Sarah Ban Breathnach

*N*othing is as difficult or as fulfilling as facing our fears of intimacy. The ability to know our own soul and share this truth with another, totally exposed and emotionally naked, is both an art and sacred act. Intimacy requires that we cultivate a relationship with both our self and God since God resides deep within our being. It's impossible to experience self-love and heartfelt closeness with another until we have walked through the illusory forest of fear and into the open field of self-love without mask or pretense. That uninhibited journey leads us into the heart and arms of unconditional love, abundance, passion and wonderment.

Once, while teaching the Self-Mastery Program, I stated that experiencing true intimacy is perhaps the most daunting work we will perform as human beings. Upon hearing this a woman in the group became uneasy and questioned, "*Intimacy*? You're saying intimacy is that important, and that hard to achieve?"

Yes. I believe intimacy is what we're all searching for. And though expressing our truth through the act of lovemaking can be a pathway to spiritual and emotional growth, true intimacy isn't about sex. It's quite possible to be deeply intimate with another and never take your feet off the floor. Genuine intimacy far surpasses the act of sex.

Anyone can remove their clothes, but few can strip away layer upon layer of fear and say, without words, "Here I am in my purest form; willing to stand before you without inhibition or disguise."

If we are to experience the oneness we long for with others, we must plunge into the waters of our own soul and release our fears. This is no small feat! Carl Jung taught that each of us has an "ideal" perception of our self, and that we will repress whatever we think, say, or do that is not congruent with this ideal perception. What does this mean for you and me? It means that much of what we feel about ourselves is going to get squelched. For fear causes us to avoid looking at ourselves, at our issues, and anything else we don't want to see. Fear is so insidious that it even has the ability to keep us from looking at the fear itself! That's why so many of us do not remember our nightly dreams. When someone asks, "Why can't I remember my dreams?" I'll remind them that their subconscious is rich with information and will gladly share it, but only to the extent one is ready to see it. If you are unwilling to look at what you are afraid of, you have a lesser chance of remembering what your subconscious conveyed to you the night before. Thus, in order for you to remember your dreams and observe the issues in your life, you must be willing to receive them along with their meaningful messages.

Dreams speak to us symbolically in the language of metaphor. For example, dreams containing bedrooms or beds are significant symbols of intimacy. When you dream of these potent metaphors, look at what is going on in your relationships. Are you desiring to bond more deeply with another but afraid to expose yourself? Is your attachment to outcome preventing you from connecting in a meaningful and heartfelt manner? Are you more worried about what others might think of you rather than being true to yourself?

Once we are willing to look at our blocks to intimacy, we will start to enjoy the splendor of real oneness and depth. Superficial conversations, encounters and relationships will become intolerable. When we have breathed life into our magnificent soul and known its bliss, we will never be satisfied with the shallow breathing of our fearful ego in quite the same manner again.

It's important to remember that our ego—that aspect which breathes and lives on fear and bases its identity upon our personality, accomplishments, body, etc.—doesn't want us to be intimate. In fact, it will do everything it can to *stop* us from being open. To the ego, intimacy is death. Avoiding issues, concerns and fears is one of the greatest barriers to intimacy in relationship. Would your ego rather you not talk about what you're really thinking and feeling? Would it prefer that you remain distant and hide from your partner behind some protective wall? You bet it would! Anything to stop a genuine and heartfelt connection from occurring.

True intimacy means being honest with your self and others, detaching from outcome, and letting go of the need to look outside your self for approval. As we remain authentic and fully present, the ego dissolves. Releasing our need to be what others want us to be, along with the belief that we are not good enough *just as we are,* disrobes the flimsy and fearful clothes of the ego. And what remains is the brilliant, lovable creation we were born to be.

Many of us have learned to be "people pleasers." The need to please others stems from low self-esteem and creates a self-destructive mask to hide behind. We believe that if we're nice, others will be less likely to reject us. In theory, this may work for a while. But if you desire meaningful and fulfilling relationships, pleasing others *won't work,* at least, not for long. We cannot love someone we do not know. And others cannot love us if we're content hiding behind a façade.

Behaving so others will like us causes us to compromise who we are. It precludes us from being real which is the basis of intimacy. Being "nice," agreeing with others, stifling who we are, not speaking our truth—all of these traits are based on fear rather than love. And fear is intimacy's greatest obstacle. There is nothing wrong with being nice to others. Yet being authentic—not from fear but from genuine self-love—is much more healing and empowering.

I know many people-pleasers and can spot them easily because I used to be one myself. Going the "extra mile" to satisfy former bosses was at the top of my people-pleasing list. I gave away much of my power to the men I worked for, driving myself beyond what was expected merely to gain their approval. Rather than appreciating myself, I looked to them for validation. Once I realized that this authority-pleasing pattern actually stemmed from wanting to please my father, I was able to release it and take my power back. The underlying fear (and all people pleasing patterns stem from fear) was that an authority figure (symbolizing my father) would get mad (causing fear to surface) and would reject me if I didn't behave according to his or her expectation (producing even more fear!).

Cultivating intimacy involves an honest and complete "fear inventory." For example, until I became conscious of what was motivating me to be "nice," I wasn't able to dismantle it. Throughout most of my life, I had no idea that I wanted to be liked for reasons that stemmed from fear of rejection. I truly thought pleasing others was the right thing to do. Also, I abhorred conflict. Wanting to be a "peacemaker" motivated me to do almost anything to prevent another from being upset. Yet as I released what was not authentically me, I realized conflict was inevitable and that I needed only to be concerned with living my truth and taking responsibility for my own reaction. I also realized that I was not responsible for how another reacted, only how I chose to react. In the book *Your Sacred Self* Wayne Dyer reminds us, "I want to make it clear that peace is not the absence of conflict. There will always be conflict because there will always be others who want you to behave as they dictate."

Ask yourself, "When do I behave in response to someone else's expectations rather than behaving in ways that feel right to me?" "Do I want to be in relationships with people who feel I am 'nice,' rather than authentic?" "What is more important to me, being liked or being loved?" "Am I willing to wear a mask in the hopes of not being rejected, or am I ready to expose my deepest self in the knowing it will build personal integrity and peace of mind?" In 1890, author Elizabeth Cady Stanton expressed,

> *Your soul longs for you to journey deep within to find the compelling answers to these questions. The moment we begin to fear the opinions of others and hesitate to tell the truth that is in us...the divine floods of light and life no longer flow into our souls.*

Remember that your ego reacts positively to superficiality, for that is what it is. Your soul, on the other hand, responds lovingly to impassioned openness and profound genuineness, for that is what *it* is. When you feel moved by a songwriter's poetic lyrics or an artist's pastoral painting, it is because your soul is connecting with the sincerity of that creator. Something in the music or art has captured the essence of your own being. Intuitively, you always know when someone is coming from their heart and demonstrating the courage to be raw and real.

Right now, take a few moments to notice your own blockages to intimacy. Can you identify a few? Seeking outside yourself for fulfillment, diverting away from your deepest self, keeping busy much of the time, not spending time alone with yourself, creating barriers to avoid connecting deeply with others, not speaking your truth, trying to please others—all of these patterns lead you away from genuine intimacy and toward unfulfilling relationships, including the relationship with yourself. Yet, by recognizing these patterns, you give yourself an opportunity to choose differently, and thus, to begin the invaluable process of healing and experiencing the intimate life.

One of my favorite lessons in *A Course in Miracles* states, "My salvation comes from me. It cannot come from anywhere else." Believing that your happiness will emanate from anything outside of you is an illusion and one of the biggest lies our society teaches us. Everywhere you look you will see something that is demanding your attention; commercials, movies, magazines, TV, love songs, and so on—externals which are merely seductive devices, created from the falsehood that they possess the power and substance to satisfy your bodily appetites. And yet your soul withers from such temptations for it knows that nothing less than the truth, nothing less than love, is worthy of you. The Course continues, "The seeming cost of accepting today's idea is this: It means that nothing outside yourself can save you; nothing outside yourself can give you peace. But it also means that nothing outside yourself can hurt you, disturb your peace or upset you in any way."

The genuinely intimate life requires giving up our "guilty secrets" and revealing the depths of who we are. We all possess depth, but few of us dare to access it. Doing so means taking responsibility and giving up the game of playing small and weak. It also means healing any shame and guilt we are hiding within the darkened corridors of our mind. My own greatest healing has always come from sharing my deepest, darkest secrets with another who was fully present and loving. Jesus said: "For where two or three are gathered together in my name, there am I in the midst of them." Nothing breaks down barriers to intimacy more quickly than coming out with the truth. That's why sharing your deepest secrets in the presence of a trusted friend, lover or counselor is such a cathartic and transforming experience.

For example, once while counseling a couple on relationship intimacy, a woman shared how she had been suppressing a painful incident that had occurred years ago with a former spouse. She harbored significant guilt over the situation and her concealing it prevented her from connecting intimately with her current partner. It not only affected their ability to honestly communicate, but their sexual intimacy as well. As she tearfully and openly shared her secret, I witnessed her partner tenderly reach for her hand. His eyes were unwavering and brimming with love as she courageously expressed herself. Afterwards, she breathed a gigantic sigh of relief and stated that a huge burden had been lifted from her heart. Healing and heartfelt, the experience bonded the couple more deeply than ever before.

A Course in Miracles reminds us we need only be willing to bring our fears out of the darkened recesses of our mind and into the light to be transformed. "Little child, you are hiding your head under the cover of the heavy blankets you have laid upon yourself. You are hiding your nightmares in the darkness of your own false certainty, and refusing to open your eyes to look at them…Take off the covers and look at what you are afraid of. Only the anticipation will frighten you, for the reality of nothingness cannot be frightening…If you will look, the Holy Spirit will judge truly. Yet He cannot shine away what you keep hidden…."

This compelling truth reminds me of a friend who shared how he used to be an "in the closet spiritual seeker." Having been raised in a conservative Christian environment, he felt his spiritual quest was unacceptable to several family members so he kept his path well hidden. While continuing the pilgrimage of his soul, he desired to write a book about his life. As he was on the precipice of publishing the book, he felt compelled to be honest with his family about his spirituality and likened the process to "coming out of the closet."

Not surprisingly, he stated the experience deepened his compassion for gay and lesbian persons who have been, or are, secretive about their sexuality. His willingness to be honest and live from his truth was the missing ingredient his soul had longed for. It empowered him to move forward in grace, strengthened his sense of self, and allowed him to be an exceptional role model for others.

What do you need to bring out of the closet? When you think of your life experiences, where do you feel the strongest twinge of regret or guilt? Being willing to look at these areas will help restore integrity and empowerment into every area of your life. The personal freedom that comes from being honest with yourself will liberate you beyond your greatest expectations.

Exploring your soul and revealing it with utmost realism is akin to an exquisite musical composition, or opus, imbued with ecstasy, harmony and wonderment. Coming home to your deepest most intimate self and sharing it with others surpasses anything else on this earth. It is of God and why we are here. What could possibly be more exciting than *that*? In the CD "A Gift of Love," 13th century poet Jalaleddin Rumi confesses his passion for intimacy with his own soul and God in the captivating words from *Looking for Your Face*:

> *Your fragrant breath like the morning breeze has come to the stillness of the garden;*
> *You have breathed new life into me.*
> *I have become Your sunshine and also Your shadow.*
> *My soul is screaming in ecstasy; every fiber of my being is in love with You;*
> *Your effulgence has lit a fire in my heart and You have made radiant*
> *for me the earth and sky.*
> *My arrow of love has arrived at the target,*
> *I am in the house of mercy and my heart is a blaze of prayer.*

RECOGNIZING YOUR SOUL

Your soul is not a passive or a theoretical entity that occupies a space in the vicinity of your chest cavity. It is a positive, purposeful force at the core of your being. It is that part of you that understands the impersonal nature of the energy dynamics in which you are involved, that loves without restrictions and accepts without judgment.

Gary Zukav, *Seat of the Soul*

*D*elving deeply into our soul leads us to experiencing profoundly rich intimacy with ourselves and others. It requires a passionate willingness that surpasses any pragmatic process or method. Sinking into your soul occurs in the unplanned moments, those "blips" between the unemotional thoughts of the intellect and the fearful concerns of the mind. When the adult intellect in all of its methodical fury ceases to plan, think, say or do, the soul can open up and exhale "ahh." The soul reveals itself in the relaxed moments, the instants when we take the opportunity to breathe deeply after days, weeks, *years* of shallow breathing, the times when we are not diverted by responsibilities, tasks or the protocol of daily living.

Routines, structured schedules, the same stuff day in and day out, are the ingredients for a very satisfied ego but a *very unfulfilled human being*. Our soul thrives when listening to the passionate lyrics in a song, witnessing the exquisite beauty of a sunrise, or feeling the silken pine needles scattered across the forest's floor. It always

resonates with what is natural, authentic—*real.*
Don't you? While attending a presentation, would
you rather listen to someone who sounds
"rehearsed" and is saying what she thinks you want
to hear, or to someone who is talking from her
heart, from what she is feeling deep within? Your
soul would prefer the latter—each and every time.

Your soul possesses the architectural
blueprint of what is most cherished. It has within it
the very threads that weave together your sacred
contract's tapestry. It knows, more than your most
intimate playmate, what will make you feel alive.
But this doesn't always mean you will feel "happy."
Soul energy encompasses the entire emotional
spectrum: nostalgia, melancholy, bitter-sweetness,
passion, tender love, longing, desire—some of the
feelings that unfortunately, we often try to suppress.
Many of the finest paintings, books, poems, plays
and songs have been born out of someone's "dark
night of the soul."

Dark nights are not pleasant, nor are they
designed to be. They occur from squelching what
we feel, from compromising who we are merely so
we can conform to someone else's mediocre
standard. After years (oops—my fingers had a
Freudian slip and mistakenly typed tears) of closing
the lid on who we are, we eventually weaken and let
our guard down. And that's when the soul emerges!
Carpé diem! Like a detective breaking open a case,
it waits for an opening and seizes the opportunity.
At last it has a porthole in which to squeak through.
And after years of having been ignored, it may feel
a little, well, a little dark. The darkness, though, is

only the pain from having cast a veil over our beloved's face. Tears inevitably spring forth when we realize we are not living the life we were born to live—tears that cleanse and heal, nourish and awaken, so we may start once again. When we accept our soul as the best part of us, then it does become our beloved and we can no longer afford the spiritual pain of ignoring it. Mary Manin Morrissey once wrote,

> *St. John of the Cross coined the phrase, "the dark night of the soul." It's a time when our soul has already disconnected from the kind of life we've been living, but we just haven't caught up with the change. So we keep trying to live our old life, only to find it doesn't work anymore. When we enter the dark night, we can find an even deeper way to communicate with God. Over time, we come to find a spirit in us that is greater than any circumstance, and we triumph over the dark.*

Within your soul dwells aliveness, the very feeling of life itself. What could possibly be more important than *that*? Would you rather live a life that is "safe" and predictable, or one in which you feel alive and real? When my life becomes a little ho-hum amidst the world's din, I remind myself "zeal is real," meaning somewhere, somehow, I have allowed my ego to usurp my soul's passion. Recognizing I can only reclaim it with conscious intention, I know I must silently declare that I am ready to surrender once again so I may return to my birthright of aliveness, joy and authenticity.

Our soul speaks to us through our feelings, desires and preferences. Yet, so many of us are numbing ourselves to what we feel. We try to block our feelings, particularly pain, from the insidious belief that we should avoid, at all costs, any discomfort. But we are mistaken when we do this, for it is our attempt at *escaping* the pain that keeps it tightly locked in place. In previous times, we did not have the appropriate tools for healing our pain. But now, as we continue blossoming into the effulgent creations we were born to be, the means for vigorously transforming our wounds into enlightening assets are being provided. Our greatest challenges are the breeding ground for our spiritual advancement. All of our experiences can be used on behalf of the greater good of others so everyone may achieve his or her greatest potential.

My mother, who passed away years ago, was a creative woman with a gregarious personality. Yet she was in a lot of pain. Not knowing how to address her pain (there weren't support groups or self-improvement books/programs/tapes back then), she took "pain pills" (ironic, isn't it?) in an attempt to relieve her suffering. When the pills failed to work, she resorted to enhancing their effect with alcohol. Over the years, I saw a dynamic and caring person wither away. Not surprisingly, her pain did not diminish one iota from the use of prescribed "pain pills." In fact, it only increased. As I grew, I watched this talented and sensitive person, whom I knew to be a great soul, become an inanimate object, too numb to know what she had to offer life and what life had to offer her.

We cannot, nor should not, escape pain. Pain is not the problem. Pain is a potent spiritual and emotional compass, reminding us where we need to correct our course. If we're suffering from a miserable relationship, unfulfilling job, or deteriorating health, then we need to reassess our situation, shift our perception and take a different route. If our pain stems from our past, then we need to be willing to seek help in releasing it.

It's important we remember the very pain we seek to escape is the same pain we need to address and heal so transformation may occur. Just as it's rare to witness a full rainbow until after it has rained, it is impossible to experience your inner light until you have released the darkness from your pain and made the choice for happiness.

All emotions have energetic "charges" which dwell in our body. Pain must be brought to the surface so we can feel its charge and say, "I am willing to release this. I no longer need this in my life. I am gaining nothing from keeping it." *A Course in Miracles* teaches, "Healing is accomplished the instant the sufferer no longer sees any value in pain. Who would choose suffering unless he thought it brought him something, and something of value to him?" Once we are ready to let go of the pain, the healing process begins.

Healing may occur cathartically via crying, beating a pillow, or screaming, or, it may happen through journaling, talking with a trusted friend, praying or meditating. Whatever form it needs to take, Spirit will direct us. We need only demonstrate a heartfelt willingness that states with conviction, "I'm ready. I'm really ready, God." Know that pain need not be a constant force in your life. Like my mother, many mistakenly believe pain is an inevitable factor. Nothing is farther from the truth. You can let go of pain and embrace love and happiness instead. Again, it's a choice.

The word "recognize" means to "know again." Thus, to recognize your soul infers that on some level, you already know it, for it has, and always will, dwell deep inside of you. Sadly, through the course of everyday living, most of us lose touch with this sacred aspect. And it's no wonder. Learning about our soul is not considered a high priority in this society. Therefore, taking the time to recognize your soul is akin to taking the necessary time to meditate. Not enough time in the day? Not a high priority? Think again. Without soul in your life, your day-to-day living becomes nothing short of a soul-*less* existence. Yuck. What a depressing thought. We've all seen places, things, and people that are lacking soul. Take the example of new construction—endless new homes are popping up in subdivisions overnight, subdivisions that are treeless (not to mention, bird-less), where the grass is "sprayed" on and every home looks like the one next to it. It reminds me of the movie *Edward Scissorhands*. And the interiors aren't much better. Like cardboard, the walls are thin and the architecture is stale and predictable. No secret passageways or hidden rooms like homes of the past. Development has made housing similar to eating at a fast food franchise: it's being done quick and cheap, unless of course, you count the staggering cost it's having upon our collective soul.

You can see the "no-soul" mentality everywhere: movies, clothes, and food. We are a "I want it fast, cheap and easy" society. Yet these lazy approaches serve only to prostitute us, for they will never warm our soul.

Cultivating intimacy requires listening to, and feeding our soul. Like our relationship with God, it calls for devotion and patience. It's the process of creation unfolding. Should you desire to create a beautiful sculpture, you would not expect to merely mold the clay a few times then presto—a gorgeous image emerges. Greatness, like a soulful life, involves persistence, willingness, and fortitude. It entails taking the time to nurture your soul as you would a beloved flower garden or pet.

In her essay "Soul Moments," Jungian analyst Marion Woodman shares,

> *If we fail to nourish our souls, they wither, and without soul, life ceases to have meaning...The creative process shrivels in the absence of continual dialogue with the soul. And creativity is what makes life worth living.*

If you want to join more deeply with your soul, you must first accept that you have a soul and then ask yourself, "What is important to my soul?" One way to accomplish this is to listen, really listen, to your thoughts, feelings and spoken words. When you are speaking to a loved one, allow yourself to hear what your soul is saying. Notice the tone behind the words. Your soul longs for you to listen and feel what it's saying. Who you're really listening to is *yourself*, the deepest part of your being.

If you desire more soul in your relationships, practice suspending judgment and commit to hearing—*really* hearing—what someone else's soul is expressing through their words, tone and non-verbal gestures. In a workshop I co-teach with my husband titled *"Cultivating the Intimate Life"* we teach couples to listen to what their partner is saying, not with their intellect, not with their ears, but with their heart and soul. Listening to the tone and inflection of their words and the energy contained within them teaches them to identify and hear the soul within the other.

Each of us has a soul, complete with unique preferences, quirks and language. The key is to tune into the soulful lyrics that exist beyond the words. As we practice hearing the soul speak in another, we come to know the desires, thoughts and feelings of our own ageless soul.

My soul communicates its heartfelt messages most clearly at night. Late at night, when all is quiet and luna's healing energy is shining through my window, I have the most opportune time to listen to what my soul has been longing for me to hear. I have come the closest to my soul just before leaving soul-less relationships and jobs, embarking on my journey of healing, revealing my deepest self to those I love, and creating artistic pieces of work via painting, writing and music. I always sense a major change is about to occur when my soul-connection intensifies. Feelings of vulnerability, excitement then fear inevitably surface, signals that I am "on my way." *Where* I'm going is not always clear. I just know I'm on the precipice of experiencing yet another dimension of my soul's wondrous destiny.

Our void is filled when our tenacious personality yields to our loving soul. The memory of why we've been born is restored and we no longer need to "do" as much as simply "be." We can be in the quiet, alone with our self, completely fulfilled. The soul, richly imbued with its endless memories from lives gone past, is ever so compelling. It becomes a comfortable magnet we gladly stretch toward as we are welcomed in its ancient and familiar embrace.

It's the heart afraid of dying, that never learns to dance;
It's the dream afraid of waking, that never takes a chance;
It's the one who won't be taken, who cannot seem to give;
And the soul afraid of dying that never learns to live.
Bette Midler, *The Rose*

EXERCISE: *COMING FACE-TO-FACE WITH YOUR SOUL*

Creating a soulful life entails capturing the essence of your soul. Many activities can inspire the song of your soul: listening to music that awakens deep emotion, digging and planting in the dirt, driving down country roads with the windows open, inhaling the scent of freshly mowed grass, walking in the summer's rain, making snow angels, lying in the arms of someone you love. The list goes on and on and most likely includes some places and activities that you also enjoyed as a child. And why wouldn't it? Our childlike selves were not as inundated with routine stresses, and thus, in some ways, they were (and are) more in tune with what was real and meaningful.

Other ways to learn more about your soul is to take a long walk—*alone*—in nature; near the water, in the woods, along the beach. *Where* you walk is less important than having the solitude necessary to rekindle your soul's language.

I best tap into my own soul by playing music that has special meaning. It may be a song I reveled in during an earlier time in my life. Perhaps the lyrics struck a chord during a time when I was going through a meaningful change, or while involved in an important relationship.

What, where and when does your soul call you to?

Times/Places I Feel Most Connected to My Soul:

_____

_____

_____

_____

_____

_____

_____

_____

_____

_____

PRAYER FOR GENUINE INTIMACY WITH MYSELF AND GOD...

"Dear Mother/Father God, help me to remember that within me dwells all of the light, glory and love I could ever want.   I need do nothing to make myself more valuable or brilliant than I already am; I need only to hold to the truth that I was created a light filled being whose function is to extend love to all I encounter. My worthiness has nothing to do with what I do, but everything to do with what I AM. Awaken the light that lives and breathes within us, remind us that our salvation comes from within, and help us to be the people You created us to be. And so it is...Amen."

INTIMACY WITH OTHERS

*If I have committed myself to God, I am free to
commit myself to another person in a way that
creates the deepest kind of love between
two human beings. Because my happiness is not
dependent on you, I am free to love and serve you in
the most joyous, exciting, and most
rewarding way; I am free to give you all my love
because, through my foundation in God, I know that
the more love I give, the more I have to give.*

Alan Cohen, *Rising in Love*

THE SPIRITUALLY-EMPOWERED MAN AND WOMAN

Personal power results from a balance of masculine and feminine forces. The spiritualization process—in men as well as women—is a feminization process, a quieting of the mind.

Marianne Williamson

E motional and spiritual empowerment are the keys to living an authentic and intimate life. It's impossible to be intimate with another when we feel powerless. If we do not have a strong sense of self, if we are not clear about what we value, if we do not honor and love ourselves, how can we possibly extend such qualities to another? Until we have acquired the emotional musculature it takes to heal and access our own deeper self, we cannot.

Currently, there is a new paradigm being constructed in relationship that involves what I refer to as the "spiritually-empowered man and woman." Both the empowered man and woman possess a strong and balanced feminine and masculine aspect. The healthy feminine aspect has clear values and boundaries, and is powerful enough to *hold the space for them*, no matter what others think, say or do. The healthy masculine aspect is aware of the values and boundaries the feminine possesses and is strong enough to *stand up for them*, despite the opinions of others. Observe some of our world's greatest leaders and you will see that they not only have a very lucid sense of what is important, but they also have the courage to speak truth, no matter what the price may be.

When we have weak feminine and masculine aspects, we are unclear of what is important and lack the necessary backbone to take a stand. For example, many of us were raised in environments where our mother allowed our father to handle the discipline even though she was the one observing the behavior. How many of us were warned, "Just wait until your father gets home!"?

Another illustration of a disempowered feminine and masculine aspect is the movie *Shine* where the mother sits idly by as the father beats his son unconscious. This is an extreme example, but it reveals how the weak feminine aspect *allows things to happen that are destructive* while the weak masculine aspect *acts destructively without sensitivity for the long-term effect.* As we learn to balance our femininity with our masculinity and honor *both* aspects, we become strong enough to access what we value so we can then take the appropriate action to support our values.

Unfortunately, the feminine is in need of great attention at this point in our emotional and spiritual development. So many of us identify with the masculine "doing-ness" that our masculine and feminine are currently very much out of balance. For example, it's much easier for us to operate from our intellect than from our feelings. We are comfortable analyzing, assessing, and quantifying, but put us in a situation where we feel vulnerable and watch out! We would rather get very busy doing something—anything—just to avoid our feelings. The masculine has been so revered that we have lost sight of the magnitude and transforming qualities of the feminine. Our femininity is where seeds are scattered and change begins, where we receive inner guidance, ideas, wisdom and inspiration. The feminine is the seat of the intuition and imagination. It is the place from which our creative juices "bubble up."

As a child I can remember wanting to be a boy like my brother, because I felt my dad liked him best. I also observed my mother acting like a very helpless woman and being dependent upon my father. Through my twenties and into my business career, I perceived men to be superior to women. Having little respect for women, I pushed away my own femininity—not in how I dressed, acted or looked—but in how I felt. I denied my feelings and desensitized myself to what was most important. Wanting to fit into the world of men, I remember not even discussing my daughter (who was less than five years old at the time) with my peers because I thought that would appear "weak" and "unprofessional." Looking back, I can see how I not only compromised my feelings but I allowed my soul to be violated.

In relationship, it's easy to see when two people are out of balance, for the traditional scenario reveals the female having a weak masculine aspect while the male has a concealed feminine aspect. This reveals itself as the woman feeling powerless, unable to speak her truth, and the man feeling and acting desensitized, unable to show his feelings.

To illustrate this point, Margot Anand in her book *The Art of Sexual Ecstasy* contrasts the difference in awareness between the "Unawakened Inner Man and Woman" versus the "Awakened Inner Man and Woman":

Unawakened Inner Man: [In a Woman] She never or rarely says no. She feels compelled to say yes because she fears that if she shows her real feelings, she will be rejected.
Awakened Inner Man: She risks saying no when she feels like it, because she respects herself, knows her limits, and does not feel afraid to express them.
Unawakened Inner Woman: [In a Man] Even in emotional moments he dares not cry because he thinks he will look like a sissy.
Awakened Inner Woman: When he feels vulnerable, he asks for support and allows the tears to flow.

The person who recognizes his or her wholeness accepts and embraces the union of both one's feminine qualities: nurturing, caring, supportive, sensual, sensitive, *and* one's masculine qualities: assertive, ambitious, analytical, probing and achieving.

It's when our feminine and masculine aspects are out of balance that destruction occurs. For example, some disempowered women tend to "hide" their spiritual growth from their spouses out of fear of disapproval and rejection. I find it both interesting and disturbing when women make excuses for their partners who are unwilling to address issues, or are indifferent and/or non-supportive of their wives' spiritual growth. I've heard comments range from, "My husband is an incredible man, I'm just careful not to mention my spiritual path," to, "I'm married to the most wonderful man. We have a great relationship. I just wish I could talk openly with him about my feelings but he prefers that I talk to my girlfriends about 'deep stuff.'"

The path of emotional and spiritual growth is not for women only! Men play an invaluable role in all of our lives, and it's unhealthy for women to exclude them from their development or to pretend that it doesn't matter whether or not they are willing to grow. Making excuses for a man's unwillingness to evolve is just as destructive as bashing men; it's the opposite side of the same coin. Further, denying the importance of men and their spiritual and emotional growth is the same as denying the masculine aspect within us.

On the flip side, the disempowered male adds to the deterioration of the relationship when he demonstrates a lack of expansion in his thinking and an unwillingness to address issues and open his heart. Numerous times, I have worked with couples in healing their relationship only to find the male putting on the brakes as we approach some core issues. More than once I've been told by the man that I'm, "too direct," or that he, "has nothing to address because everything is 'fine,'" (yet his partner is obviously unhappy and desiring more closeness). This reminds me of a joke I once read:

A man walking along a California beach was deep in prayer. All of a sudden he said out loud, "Lord grant me one wish." Suddenly the sky clouded above his head and in a booming voice the Lord said, "Because you have tried to be faithful to me in all ways, I will grant you one wish." The man said, "Build a bridge to Hawaii, so I can drive over anytime I want to." The Lord said, "Your request is very materialistic. Think of the logistics of that kind of undertaking, the support required to reach the bottom of the Pacific! The concrete and steel it would take! I can do it, but it is hard for me to justify your desire for worldly things. Take a little more time and think of another wish, a wish you think would honor me."

The man thought about it for a long time. Finally he said, "Lord, I have been married and divorced four times. All of my wives said that I am uncaring and insensitive. I wish that I could understand women. I want to know how they feel inside, what they are thinking when they give me the silent treatment, why they cry, what they mean when they say 'nothing' and how I can make a woman truly and genuinely happy."

After a few minutes God asks, "You want two lanes or four on that bridge?"

And though we laugh it's bittersweet because we know it's all too true. Men are taught to be indifferent and unemotional. The cost of this programming is staggering. It causes men to repress their feelings, avoid being emotionally accessible to their partner, shun their need for nurturing, and compromise who they really are. What higher price could one possibly pay?

Again, growth is not restricted to women. If you are a man who desires a meaningful, loving and passionate relationship, be willing to experience healing. This means looking within and facing your fears. Intimacy can only occur to the extent you are in touch with your deepest most authentic self. Spiritual and emotional growth is not for "sissies"; it takes guts and is the hardest work you'll ever experience.

It's also important that women recognize and accept they are whole and complete—with or without a partner. I have met many women who are unhappy in their relationships, but too afraid to leave because of their financial dependence upon their partner. And conversely, I know countless men who feel their greatest contribution is their paycheck. This is not the way of healthy and intimate relationship!

Relationships like these, and there are a lot of them, only breed resentment and a feeling of separateness. They are based on what *A Course in Miracles* calls "specialness" and stem from the belief that another can somehow "complete" us. This delusion has only caused us to create immature and egotistic relationships where our need to "get" something has drained the life force from the bond. No wonder we end up feeling empty, resentful and lonely. And yet, the Course teaches us that our relationships are the most important vehicle for healing and transformation: "The special relationships of the world are destructive, selfish and childishly egocentric. Yet, if given to the Holy Spirit, these relationships can become the holiest things on earth." As we ask Spirit to heal our relationships—all of them—we are shown how to forgive while empowering the other to be the magnificent and light-filled person they were born to be.

On a larger scale, when the feminine and masculine are not balanced, problems arise in the form of a polluted planet, starving children, abuse of women/children/men/animals, sexual violations, etc. All of these situations are a result of passive or convoluted values and boundaries (feminine) and the unwillingness to take a stand (masculine). When a man or woman is in touch with his or her heart and demonstrates the courage to act on it, healing occurs and the world is transformed.

To become spiritually empowered men and women we must first become clear of their qualities. The women and men I have met and worked with who are empowered have some very distinct traits that include the following:

SPIRITUALLY EMPOWERED WOMAN	SPIRITUALLY EMPOWERED MAN
Has faith and trust in a Higher Power; is committed to a path of personal and spiritual growth;	Has faith and trust in a Higher Power; is committed to a path of personal and spiritual growth;

Possesses clear values
and takes a stand on them;

Allows himself to feel
his feelings and express
them;

Is capable of financially sup-
porting herself; does not have
to rely on others for financial
support;

Values his worth; enjoys
his work, does not
remain in unfulfilling
job out of "sacrifice";

Speaks her truth with pure
intention;

Listens to others with
"compassionate-
objectivity";

Approves of, and respects
her body;

Approves of, and
respects his body;

Recognizes and acts on
her inner talents and gifts;

Practices open minded-
ness and non-judgment;

Appreciates her sexuality
and views herself as a
spiritually-sexual being;

Appreciates his sexual-
ity and views sex as a
means for expressing
love;

Looks for the light in
others...

Looks for the light in
others...

These are just some of the qualities
spiritually empowered women and men possess.
Ask yourself, "What do I most value? What is most
important to me?" Then ask, "Am I willing to take a
stand on my values? If my values were being
challenged, would I speak up, even if what I said

opposed what others believe? Am I strong enough to let go of what others think of me?"

As we bring our unconscious to consciousness, we become stronger and more loving people. The need to control others begins to diminish and we no longer need to seek outside ourselves for approval or recognition.

When our feminine and masculine aspects are balanced, we are not afraid to say, "*No!*" to the demolition of our environment; "*No!*" to the destructive shows and movies that commingle sex with violence; "*No!*" to the judgment and hatred exhibited toward persons of other races, religions and sexual preferences; "*No!*" to the manipulative and seductive way women are portrayed in books and movies; "*No!*" to the sexual assaults made on our female population; "*No!*" to young men being taught it's not okay to cry; "*No!*" to women being perceived as victims and men as victimizers.

William Stafford once stated, "It's important that awake people be awake, or a breaking line may discourage them back to sleep. The signals we give, 'Yes' and 'No' and 'Maybe' must be clear. The darkness around us is deep." For healing to occur we must be willing to let go of the fence walking many of us practice in our daily lives; attitudes such as "maybe," "I'll 'try,'" or "I'm not sure what my truth is," are wavering and breaking lines which enable us to remain asleep. Our heart and soul will pave the way toward balance if we are willing to keep them open and bravely declare "Yes!" to what rings of truth and "No!" to what no longer serves the whole. Now is the time to awaken and to remain awake.

Our patriarchal society is crumbling, as it should. All of us—men and women—have come to value a sophisticated, "civilized" society where high-powered technology and material comforts rule, yet we are paying a staggering price for it. In some primitive societies where the feminine joins the masculine, the focus is on feeling, being and relating with well-being, self-esteem, and community the net result. As our spirits continue to awaken, our pendulum of male and female energies will find equilibrium. The swing is heading toward a critical mass of feminine values, yet in reality, the optimum is neither patriarchal nor matriarchal, but equal balance, each in harmony with one another.

LIGHTENING THE LOAD

Forgiveness is the key to happiness.
A Course in Miracles

*I*ntimacy is impossible without forgiveness. True intimacy involves the willingness to speak our truth and create a safe, forgiving space in which to share. When we forgive someone, we clear the pathway in our heart and mind; we open new channels for love and passion to flow through; we begin anew. As long as we're hanging onto grievances or past resentments, we're incapable of fully loving and appreciating the person in the present.

I once read a story from an anonymous student that wonderfully illustrates the value of forgiveness:

> *One of my teachers had each one of us bring a clear plastic bag and a sack of potatoes. For every person we refused to forgive for whatever they did, we were told to choose a potato, write the name and date on it, and put it in the plastic bag. Some of our bags were quite heavy. We were then told to carry this bag with us wherever we went for a week or two, putting it beside our bed at night, on the car seat when driving, next to our desk at work, etc. The hassle of lugging this around with us made clear what a weight we were carrying spiritually and emotionally, and how we had to pay*

attention to it all of the time so as not to forget it and leave it in embarrassing places. Naturally, the condition of the potatoes deteriorated to a nasty slime. This was a great metaphor for the price we pay for nursing our grudges. Too often we think of forgiveness as a gift to the other person while really it is for ourselves! So the next time you decide you can't forgive someone, ask yourself, "Isn't your bag heavy enough?"

How heavy is your load? Another way to put it is: how peaceful are you? I always know when I have some forgiving to do because I will experience inner conflict, sadness, anxiety or feel just plain "out of peace." Grievances are akin to carrying chains around our shoulders, but worse. They squelch our happiness, fulfillment and hope; they crush our feelings of worthiness and self-love, and they thwart our ability to be the accepting, non-judgmental and loving beings we were born to be. *A Course in Miracles* reminds us that our pathway to inner peace can only be achieved through forgiveness. And genuine forgiveness means seeing all of the good in another and choosing to *let all the rest go*!

Genuine forgiveness has nothing to do with our over-looking someone's "sins" because we're so "holy," but everything to do with the fact that whatever someone did or didn't do is only our perception. And since our perceptions are based on the limitations of our physical senses, we are wrong whenever we judge someone. *A Course in Miracles* reminds us, "perception is a mirror, not a fact."

Forgiveness, first and foremost, is a choice. Everything is forgivable. When I hear someone say that they cannot forgive someone because that person has done "the unforgivable," it's apparent they are unwilling to let go of their anger and/or pain. Or, when a person shares, "I've tried and tried to forgive so-and-so, but it's just not happening," they really mean, "I am not yet ready to release the other person or myself from the binding chains of resentment."

Yet it's important to remember that what we give, we receive. Thus every time we condemn another we condemn ourselves. Every time we withhold forgiveness, we, in fact, withhold it from ourselves. The other person will not suffer nearly as much as we will.

Further, God does not judge us, *we* do. And since all minds are joined, we are succumbing to the temptation to put down ourselves every time we are tempted to put down another. Even if we are judging another for something we have not done, our judgment will boomerang back to us, causing us to feel guilty.

A friend once shared that she was participating in a conversation on forgiveness when some people stated how they felt they were being punished for some previous behavior. My friend, wanting to keep the peace, yet wanting to share her own perception of a loving God questioned, "But what if God doesn't judge? What if it's only *we* who judge, not God?" The room resonated with the sounds of silence. Each were convinced that they would have to face "judgment day" at one point or another so they hadn't considered the fact that maybe the only judgment they would need to heal was their *own*.

We are always our own worst critic and harshest judge. Yet when we practice forgiveness, we release others from judgment and are simultaneously released. We become free! Nothing is more liberating and exhilarating than letting go of thoughts and feelings filled with anger and resentment.

Forgiveness is the cornerstone of genuine intimacy and the key to happiness. Experiencing resentment—from the slightest twinge of annoyance to the utmost intense anger—prevents us from being in the moment. It makes it impossible to connect deeply with the person in front of us, and, since grievances are thoughts filled with energy, we are bound to focus on them whether we're conscious of it or not. Therefore, it takes more energy to retain a grievance than it does to release it.

In addition, feeling judgmental toward another separates us from that person, and therefore, separates us from God and ourselves. We cannot possibly feel safe exposing ourselves if we are feeling separate from our innermost self. It is not possible to experience the love in another if we are judging them. You can't justify, "Well, I may be upset with so-and-so, but I'm not with my partner, so what's the big deal?" The big deal is that since we are all connected, the thoughts and feelings you have toward another will inevitably carry forward into every relationship in your life, including the relationship with yourself. The mind has no way of escaping grievances. When we are willing to let go of all our "potatoes," our soul can breathe deeply from the lightness of spirit while rejoicing in the buoyancy of its lightened load.

Once, while teaching a workshop on forgiveness, a participant raised her hand and shared how she was very angry with an ex-spouse and unwilling to let him "off the hook" for the terrible things he had done. She was convinced that holding onto her anger enabled her to continue punishing him and that *someone* had to do it! After some probing, it became clear she was not ready to let go of this man and that her resentment gave her the necessary excuse for not moving forward and opening her heart in other relationships.

Spirit will assist us in releasing our heavy load if we ask. But first, we must admit we need to forgive and are willing to do so. If you have been struggling with forgiving someone, ask yourself, "What am I gaining by holding onto this resentment?" "What am I afraid will happen if I forgive this person?"

Forgiveness occurs in layers. Often we must practice forgiving the same person time and time again. Below are five steps that when practiced with sincere intention and willingness will lead to a lighter load:

1) Remind yourself that you deserve to be happy and that forgiveness is the pathway to happiness.

2) Become aware of your "potatoes"—the grievances, resentments and dislikes you are carrying. This involves lifting the veils of denial and being willing to accept that any inner conflict you experience, from minimal irritation to out and out rage, are all areas where forgiveness is needed. (Keep in mind that this part is often the hardest, for it entails allowing your true thoughts and feelings to surface. Many of us have a difficult time admitting we're angry or upset because we haven't been taught how to express these feelings appropriately. Also, we tend to judge these emotions as "negative" and thus believe that they are not "spiritual" or "nice.") Start by asking yourself, "Where am I carrying grievances against myself?" "What do I most regret?" Next, "Whom do I most need to release?" Allow thoughts, feelings, and past experiences to surface *without judgment*.

3) Ask for a "miracle" or shift in perception. Turning to God for guidance and asking, "Help me to see myself as You see me," will do this. Let feelings of sadness, regret or anger surface and then be willing to release these feelings, clearing the path for forgiveness to occur. Remind yourself that you did the best you knew how at the time and that anything you did or didn't do was because of fear, and thus, was a call for love. Lovingly affirm that whatever you've done has not changed your core essence or diminished your innocence in any way.

4) In forgiving another, focus on the kind and loving things the person did in the past. Remember that they, just like you, desire only to be loved, lovable and loving.

5) Remain willing to release your grievances and practice having faith and trust that forgiveness will occur if you allow it to.

6) Remain willing to release the past and honor yourself for being willing to forgive while enjoying your "lightened load."

The soul looketh steadily forward creating a new world before her, leaving worlds behind her.

Emerson

BEYOND THE FEAR OF INTIMACY

This is the spiritual meaning of intimacy: growth inward, past our masks and fears and recklessness, to the sacred place where we are naked before God and each other.

Marianne Williamson

*I*ntimacy can only be experienced as we learn to love ourselves (and others), not for who we think we should be, but for who we really *are*. We are constantly in process; our soul longs to move forward, to experience the richness of living life with an open mind and expanded heart, and it is only through our own soul growth that we can bring passion and intimacy into our relationships.

Author, teacher and dream analyst, Marion Woodman, shares how a common dream theme entails the dreamer being instructed to go to the basement or cellar to find a black box. As the dreamer looks into the box, she sees a bird, wispy and skeleton-like that hoarsely whispers, "I only wanted to sing my song...." How many of us have not recognized our soul's passion and/or not possessed the courage to act on it? Sadly, this dream metaphor is true for most of us. Far too many of us have come to the end of our life only to discover that we have not fulfilled our soul's destiny.

This need not be!

As we delve inward to our soul and listen to its urging, we awaken with the aliveness and passion that feeds life force energy our relationships, nourishing them with zest and excitement. When our relationships become boring and routine (yawn), it's because we are not diving within where our emotional and passionate waters run deep. In fact, when one is sexually shut down (and keep in mind that our sexual desire is where our co-creative spark surges from), it's often because we are not in touch with our soul. The physical "dryness" we may be experiencing is symbolized by the lack of creative and soulful juices that are not flowing.

Countless times, while counseling people on relationship, I hear how the sexual desire is gone for one or both parties. When this is expressed, my immediate response is, "Are you feeling emotionally close to one another?" and "Are you taking the time to do your own 'soul work'?" Quite often, the partners are not looking within to their own creative source. Each one is looking instead to the other for sustenance. If we don't plunge into our soul and connect with Spirit, we become barren, leaving us with absolutely nothing to give. It's no wonder we end up feeling unfulfilled, empty and needy!

If you desire intimacy, first look to your relationships and notice if those closest to you feel accepted and loved for who they are. Next, observe how often you are loving and accepting of yourself. Any thoughts that are self-deprecating and critical are the places where healing is needed in order for true intimacy to occur. To the extent you honor yourself and allow your own soul to soar is the same extent that you will be willing to support another's inner light and soulful flight.

Next, ask yourself, "How well do I know my own soul?" "How much time am I taking to access my passion?" "Am I willing to spend the necessary time alone to connect with my soul?"

Bringing our unconscious mind into consciousness is the stuff dreams—and healthy, intimate relationships—are made of. It's through our relationships that we discover if we are projecting our needs onto another, versus if we truly love that person. Projection occurs when we disassociate from our thoughts, feelings, desires, and fears, and see them instead, in another. For example, I may accuse my partner of being distant and withdrawn from me, when in reality, it is me who is feeling or acting distant. I often see this occur in the area of commitment where one partner is blaming the other for not being committed. How interesting it is to discover that the person wanting more commitment is the one unwilling to extend love. For real commitment involves loving another for who they are, not for who we expect them to be.

Genuine intimacy starts with *us*. We cannot give something we do not have. So, to know another means we must first know ourselves. Probing questions, such as "What does my soul crave?" "What do I most need to experience in order to grow?" and "What brings me aliveness and joy?", blaze a trail for our spiritual and emotional development.

Once we have awakened the spark within, we must be willing to release our attachment to the opinions of others and live a life that suits us, no matter how different that life may appear to be. A healed life, an empowered life, an intimate life, is foreign to us. We currently have no paradigm for true intimacy and unconditional love. Societal beliefs about relationship, being based on fear and guilt, cannot guide us. In fact, mainstream consciousness is still imbedded in the belief that form is everything and that soul growth, if there is such a thing, is irrelevant. Thus, we must be willing to forge the paths of a mature relationship on our own. This entails using the guidance of our intuition, synchronicities and assistance from our higher self.

Like a snake shedding its skin, we heal and evolve as we release old patterns and reach upward, like kundalini energy, toward our higher good. As we become more conscious, our masculine and feminine energies are ignited and the effort toward balancing these primal energies begins. Symbolically, this may be seen as two snakes simultaneously rising upward. Although in Western culture many of us fear snakes and equate them to evil and destruction, they are actually a powerful archetype representing the creative life force that flows through the endocrine centers, propelling us toward spiritual awareness. Being created with the ability to shed many skins, snakes are frequently a symbol of eternal life.

If you are ready to inflame your relationships with passion and intimacy, you must first be willing to become inspired yourself. Remember that there is a wellspring of joy and aliveness already within you. Only your willingness and desire are needed to awaken it. Once you have tapped into the Godforce energy that nourishes your soul, you will never, ever, want to settle for less. Doing so will feel like death. Your soul is eternal and thrives on experiencing the depths of life. Recognizing this fact will inspire you to relish all of the richness that a genuinely intimate and awakened life offers you.

LOVE WITHOUT LIMITS

I cannot always see the higher picture of divine order. For it is the inalienable right of all life to choose their own evolution and with great love I acknowledge your right to determine your future.
Author Unknown

*T*he word intimacy actually illustrates the heartfelt concept of "in-to-me-see." When we yearn for intimacy, it is as though we are stating, "Look into the depth of my being and see beyond the mask, beyond the personality, beyond the experiences, beyond everything that I appear to be and into the truth of who I AM."

We are offered no greater capacity to know the truth of who we really are than in relationship. Relationships are such powerful catalysts because they mirror the aspects we most need to see for our soul-growth. What we see and react to in another, we possess within ourselves. Thus the fear and love we see on our beloved's face is the reflection of both our own humanness and divinity.

Case in point: For many years my husband has told me how much he loves me and how beautiful I am. Yet for a long time, I discounted his compliments because I was so critical of myself. It wasn't until years later when I was feeling loving and lovable, that I realized he was reflecting back the love inside of me, and it was the inner love that enhanced my outer beauty. So it wasn't until I experienced *self-love* that I could believe the image shining back. Now, I no longer invalidate his admiration. In fact, I am able to receive his compliments and love with acceptance and appreciation.

Through relationship, we must lose ourselves in order to find ourselves. As we release our attachment to the form of our relationships and remain focused on the content (unconditional love), we experience what *A Course in Miracles* calls the healed or holy relationship. In order to do so, we need to *unlearn* what we've been taught about love and *relearn* what true love actually is. In our society we confuse love with "getting" something from another which is what *A Course in Miracles* refers to as "special love." Demands and expectations are forms of *sacrifice*, not love.

When, as parents, we express love for our children based on their performance, grades, clean rooms, "good" behavior—we are teaching them they are not lovable just as they are. And when, as partners, we "love" another based on the money, sex, attention they provide—we are demonstrating they are not worthwhile as the human being they are, but only for what they "give" us. Every relationship starts out a special relationship and remains so until healing has occurred. If you question whether or not your relationships are filled with specialness, ask yourself, "How much would I still appreciate my partner if he or she stopped giving me what I deem important? How much would I love him or her if he or she loved another as much as me? How long would my heart be open if he or she decided it was time to release the relationship with me and move on? Would I still 'love' him or her?"

The ego's thinking teaches us that marriage is to love another forever, but how many times have we seen relationships end in divorce, only to find both parties resenting the other? Or, how often do we marry someone only to discover that after years of living together, we have very little in common with the person who shares our bed?

While counseling others, I have witnessed the death of aliveness so often experienced in the beginning of a relationship, simply because one or both parties has become enmeshed in the *form* of the relationship. Form is anything that involves physical space and time, and its emphasis is on how the relationship "looks" and how one "behaves." The ego is in its glory when someone does something for us, or even better, gives up something for us—in our society that is considered "love." Form is antithetical to substance, or content, and offers no real or lasting sustenance to one's heart and soul. Being based on how the other person *behaves*, it cannot connect with the love inside the him or her, and so real intimacy becomes impossible to experience.

Content is genuine inner love for self and another. It's founded on the basis of abundance, not scarcity, sacrifice or specialness. Content recognizes that we were created with an infinite supply of love and that we are deprived of nothing. From this viewpoint, we do not need another to "fill us up" as though we are some empty tank of gas.

We are already complete and whole and desire only to extend our supply of love with others.

To move from "form" to "content" entails letting go of our need to be special and this can be a very painful process. We have been taught to focus on form rather than content in every area of our life. Yet in no situation is this more clearly demonstrated than in our closest relationships; what we think is love is really a need to control the behavior of our loved ones. When we control, we secure the image we want to retain of ourselves merely so we do not have to change or grow. To truly love another means loving without limits, loving wholeheartedly no matter how the other person behaves or whether or not they love us in return. It's easy to love someone when we feel they love us, big deal. It's an entirely different story when they do not act loving toward us. Forgiveness is the same; to forgive someone who is nice and loving is easy. The real test of genuine forgiveness is when someone has done something you perceive is hurtful, and they don't like you and probably never will. How easy is it to forgive them then?

I have been blessed with being able to witness the releasing of attachment to form and the opening to genuine love and intimacy within my own marriage. My husband, Tom, and I are students of *A Course in Miracles*, and an invaluable part of our healing pathway involves recognizing and healing our specialness through forgiveness. From time to time, we encounter "opportunities for growth" disguised as challenges that enable us to dissolve our attachment to how we think things *should be* (form), into what our hearts tell us they *really are* (content). This has entailed a lengthy and intense process of letting go of what society deems important in relationship including the patriarchal thinking that dominates our culture.

Interestingly, our learning process of loving without limits peaked during a time when I fell in love with another person while married to Tom. Though I love Tom deeply, during this particular time, I found that I loved another, too. Of course, this flew in the face of everything we had been taught about "normal" and traditional relationship. How could I love my husband and another, too? "Why," my ego insisted, "there must be something wrong, here. You cannot love two people at the same time!" Adding to my confusion was the fear of teaching several spiritually oriented workshops and leading discussions in which I felt most of the participants would never understand what I was feeling or going through. Deep in my heart, loving this person felt very right, very real. And, it did not diminish my love for Tom one iota. Yet I feared that my feelings were "wrong" and that others would judge me.

It dawned on me that my spiritual growth was the reason this experience was occurring. Because of my soulful pilgrimage, I had asked for assistance in learning to love myself and others without reservation. Well, from this particular situation I received the opportunity to learn the lesson, for the love I felt toward both people threw my evolutionary journey into a whole new velocity. For years, Tom and I had professed our love for each other and felt we had built a strong and loving foundation. Then years later, here we were confused about what was happening to our sacred relationship. I felt both perplexed and intrigued that I deeply cared for another, while Tom felt scared and bewildered over losing what he had come to know and expect within our relationship.

One of Tom's greatest fears was losing an aspect of our relationship that made him feel secure. This situation was creating a change in the form of our relationship, and as painful as it was, it was also the catalyst for much healing. Tremendous amounts of jealousy surfaced, and during much of the process, we felt as though we were on an emotional roller coaster. Enormous guilt surfaced within me, for how could I possibly cause pain to someone I loved so profoundly? And yet, on a deeper level, I also knew that this was a breakthrough opportunity for me to accept what was in my heart, and, to have faith in Tom as a strong and light-filled soul who had the capacity to lovingly work through the issue with me. Of course, fear was everywhere and it shouted to Tom, "How can you allow this to happen? What kind of man are you, anyway? Why, you should give her an ultimatum! Either she wants you or she's out of here!" And of course, society's fear-based belief system would have provided endless support for his ego, as it appeared Tom was indeed a "victim."

My own fear-ridden ego warned, "How selfish of you, it's not spiritual of you to love two people, can't you see what it's doing to them? This will ruin your career; no one will ever understand how you could equally love two people at the same time. In this monogamous society, it's unacceptable, especially when you're married!" From mainstream consciousness I certainly seemed to be playing the ultimate archetypal role of "victimizer."

For me, the options seemed to be: 1) Shut my heart down to the other person and love Tom "exclusively"; 2) Divorce Tom so the legal marital contract no longer bound us to such confining form; or, 3) Open our hearts and minds to healthier alternatives that empowered us and allowed the relationship to expand and grow rather than constrict and die. Through the strength of God, we chose the latter. In the short run, it appeared that it would have been much easier for Tom to close his heart down. But, both of us knew the painful consequence of that choice. Thus, not only did he choose to keep his heart open, he began the arduous task of practicing unconditional love. Likewise, it appeared that it would have been far less complicated for me to shut down my own heart to both him and the other person. Yet, I felt a loving and deep bond with each person that could only be described as a soulful one. In my heart, I knew that keeping my love flowing and working through the situation was the most healing thing to do.

Throughout this life transforming process, I became very clear that my soul felt compelled to open to another human being so that opportunities for healing could occur. From a higher standpoint, my soul was only interested in the growth that was occurring. It didn't care about what it looked like to others, or if we were doing it "right." Its only concern was for the unfolding of our hearts and the ability to love each other during this challenging and confusing time. This realization reminded me of a healing quote I once read from Joan Borysenko, Ph.D., in *Ensouling Ourselves* which affirmed:

> *Some tension is necessary for the soul to grow, and we can put that tension to good use. We can look for every opportunity to give and receive love, to appreciate nature, to heal our wounds and the wounds of others, to forgive, and to serve... Growth of the soul is our goal, and there are many ways to encourage that growth, such as through love, nature, healing our wounds, forgiveness, and service. The soul grows well when giving and receiving love. I nourish my soul daily by loving others and being vulnerable to their love. Love is, after all, a verb, an action word, not a noun.*

I realized I could either experience this situation within the marriage if it were fluid enough to allow for it, or outside the marriage via separation or divorce if it was not. I began to shift my perception to accept that the form of our relationship may change and that genuine love and friendship was more important than a marriage that lacked real honesty and total acceptance. At the same time, Tom became willing to release his attachment to the form he had become accustomed to, and instead, practice loving me as he would a very dear friend.

We discovered that as we remained committed to being completely honest and open with each other (not an easy task when one is feeling guilty and afraid!), our confusion of love with expectation, control, and sacrifice surfaced for healing.

During this process, Tom meditated on accessing the inner strength and courage it required to "unlearn" what his ego thought relationship should "look" like. The pseudo-masculine belief that he should not put up with such unacceptable behavior and that I was his "wife/possession" began to dissolve as he relied upon higher guidance for direction and inner fortitude. He learned the invaluable lesson of detaching from the opinion of others and to follow the love in his heart. This also led him to opening himself to the other person while embracing their humanness and divinity. Though this was an experience that brought out some of Tom's darkest emotions, he learned the priceless lesson of loving another without conditions. Interestingly, during this same time, the anonymously written and moving passage *A Definition of Unconditional Love* was given to us which summed up our situation perfectly:

> *I love you as you are as you seek to find your own special way to relate to the world, or the way you feel that is right for you. It is important that you are the person you want to be and not someone that others or I think*

you should be. I realize that I cannot know what is best for you although perhaps sometimes I think I do. I've not been where you have been, viewing life from that angle. I do not know what you have chosen to learn or how you have chosen to learn it, with whom, or in what time period. I have not walked life looking through your eyes so how can I know what you need?

Undeniably, the unfolding of this experience led to necessary and unsurpassable healing and intimacy for all three of us. It equally challenged our willingness and ability to demonstrate unconditional love, not from denial, but through loving and supportive acceptance. All of us were on the same pathway of healing and very familiar with the ego's attachment to form. We recognized our salvation stemmed from keeping our hearts open and looking for the light and love in each other.

There was no deception, no guilty secrets. Each of us committed to building a comfortable context for sharing, while remaining honest despite our anxiety. We learned to create a safe space in which to share our thoughts, feelings and fears, something we knew our souls longed for.

Being willing and able to let go of the form of our relationship allowed my own soul to soar. I felt accepted for who I was, not for how I behaved. Tom's soul thrived from giving him the gift of freedom. Letting go of what his ego deemed threatening, but what his higher self knew to be true, was the ultimate experience of loving unconditionally which simply reflected his own capacity for self-love.

THE POWER OF LOVE

There comes a time we all know, there's a place that we must go, into the soul, into the heart, into the dark.
                    Melissa Etheridge, CD *Breakdown*

*A*s previously mentioned, soul growth entails embracing the entire spectrum of what life offers—from birth to change, metamorphosis to death, letting go to yet another rebirth. Each soulful step requires the leap of faith from knowing we are marching toward higher ground. Who among us has not experienced this ever-unfolding process in our relationships? For relationships, as *A Course in Miracles* reminds us, are "temples" for the Holy Spirit to work through. They are a hothouse for major transformation to occur both emotionally and spiritually.

Each of us possesses a soul that has incarnated with specific tasks and experiences to achieve in this lifetime. And it is within our relationships that our soul evolves the quickest. How? By learning to open our heart and lower the walls of defense that tower around this vital love-pumping instrument. By practicing forgiveness and appreciating all of the love we ever gave and received. By having faith and trust that all of our relationships are "assignments" which possess the power to take us closer to God. So…why do we feel such a need to guard our heart and from where does this fear-based motivation stem? On one hand, all of us desire intimacy, to expose our deepest selves and be emotionally naked with another. Since the Godforce energy resides deep within each of us, connecting intimately eliminates any sense of separation. Connecting with another nourishes our soul with euphoria, acceptance and unconditional love. On the other hand, as our relationships mature, fear surfaces, and we frequently feel we are hitting against an invisible yet prominent "wall." The initial elation transforms into nothing short of frustration. Now the question becomes, "Where did the love go?"

Our soul thrives in relationship, even during the most challenging times because our encounters with others are our greatest opportunities for growth. When people come to me for counseling and complain, "I need help in addressing this problem," I'm apt to state, "Let's reframe 'problem' into 'growth opportunity,' okay? It will be much easier for you to move through this process if you recognize issues as learning experiences, for that is what they are."

When we show up in relationship and are fully present, our soul soars from the human feelings we experience. But though our soul may love it, our fearful ego may not. It's not easy opening our heart to another especially if we have been hurt in the past. Like a wounded animal, our natural tendency is to protect ourselves by either shutting down our heart or guarding it with sheltering layers. Either way, since we get what we give, we only end up cutting ourselves off from our own flow of love as well as the love from others. In my own life I've discovered that nothing is more painful than blocking love's flow. Though my ego warns, "Protect yourself, don't be too vulnerable or you're going to get hurt!" (sound familiar?), I know it's just fear speaking and if I listen to this voice, I will hurt even *more*.

Within us dwell two voices, offering two choices. One voice is the fear-ridden ego, forever seeking to protect and preserve itself, while the other Voice is the compassionate love of Spirit, desiring only to heal and replace our pain with unconditional love and joy. The goal, then, is to ask for guidance and listen to the Voice for Love, for if we don't the issue remains, "How to trust so we can love without reservation?"

This question reminds me of a comment a friend once made about trusting her husband and keeping her heart open to him. Since she had been hurt in a previous marriage, she felt her heart could not handle more of the same. In order to protect herself, she kept herself very busy with work, friends and family to avoid intimacy with her husband. She felt that keeping busy helped her in not being so hypersensitive. Around that same time, another dear friend shared some healing words of wisdom about loving without limits from the Circle of Atonement in Sedona, Arizona:

> *Because I believe love has limits, I have come to be afraid of it: afraid it will be withdrawn, afraid of its conditions, afraid that what seems to be love is only a tease, a tantalizing promise that threatens to disappear if I misbehave. That fear, that*

constant anxiety over love's potential for disappearance is the source of my lack of joy. How can I be joyful, even when things are "good," if love may be withdrawn at any moment? This is the error of our minds we are practicing to uncover, bring to the light, and let go of. Right now, in this moment, I am encircled by His embrace. Right now, without a single thing changing, the Love of God radiates to me without limit and without reservation or question. To know this is happiness, and it is this I seek today.

These words speak of the fears we must face, the place where we must go into the soul, into the heart, into the dark, where we believe love has limits and will be withdrawn. As we face this demon, this fear-saturated monster perched upon our shoulder shouting, "Watch out, protect yourself!", we can choose to release ourselves from the intimacy-blocking shackles chaining us. Rereading the above heartfelt words of wisdom reminds me how true this message is for all of us. Love is eternal; we need not fear losing the love of another.

Abandonment, rejection, withdrawal—these kinds of gut-wrenching fears are only part of the illusion. In truth, the issue is, we are rejecting and abandoning ourselves. *For the only real pain we will ever feel stems from withholding our love.* In reality, all love already resides within us. And since we have an infinite wellspring from which to give, how could we ever truly be without love? This reminds me of a beautiful quote I once read from an anonymous source that affirmed, "You can never lose by loving; you can only lose by holding back."

In my own life, I am frequently tempted to shelter my heart and take the "safe" route. Deep inside, however, I know I must take risks, keep my love flowing, and have faith that all experiences are yet another doorway for my soul. In fact, I realize that if I don't walk through the doorway, I will return to the same painful place again and again. I cannot love another and not be changed by the experience. Every opportunity leads me to pastures where my soul can graze and gain sustenance while propelling me beyond my highest expectations.

For example, while writing this book I felt a strong need to dig deeply within myself. I kept thinking, "How can I write a book about intimacy unless I am willing to be intimate with my own soul?" And for me, being intimate requires solitude. In fact, I found I desired more time alone during the creation of this book than ever before. Because of the soulful space I needed, my husband, Tom, sometimes felt pushed away and confused by my behavior. While finishing the remaining 20% of *The Intimate Soul*, I felt myself becoming even more distant. This, of course, was very challenging for Tom, and after a particularly trying couple of months, he felt our connection was akin to a cord whose strands were gradually "breaking." I thought the distance we were experiencing was merely a result of my writing, but on a deeper level, I sensed

I was unconsciously beginning to use writing as a means to inhibit intimacy.

Looking back, I can see that I was actually creating what I was defending against. What better way for my ego to block me from writing a book on intimacy than to keep me from experiencing it in my own life? There were many nights I remember falling asleep after an evening of writing and hearing my ego chide, "You can't be serious! How can you possibly write about this subject if you're not even practicing it yourself?" In truth, my soul didn't care one iota if I wrote about intimacy, it only desired that I *felt it*, *tasted it*, and *knew it* in every part of my life. During this period while feeling confused and uncertain of what to do next, I received an e-mail from Tom one day titled "*Passion*":

My Dearest Laura,

I would like to say that I love you with all my heart. I know that I may lack passion in some areas of my life, but, Laura, when it comes to you and our relationship, I have all the passion that God has given me. The strands of our bond maybe be stretching, and maybe some have broken, but there still remains a very strong connection. And, for those strands that have broken, I will mend them with all my heart and soul. Because, I want you, I want you very much. Until you tell me it's no use, I will not give up. I have come to believe in "us" with such faith that nothing but ourselves can do us under. I want to give you the kind of love that you deserve. And, I am willing to make whatever changes necessary to promote real love. If I thought I couldn't do that I would tell you. My Higher Self is telling me I can and my ego is having a fit. I honor you as a beautiful soul deserving of unconditional love and I would like to grow and evolve with you. My heart leaps at the thought of being intimately connected to your heart. Yes, I know you've heard all this before. But, each time I fail I come back stronger and more committed. Your frustration is not lost on me. I get it. I will give you the space you need and whatever else that honors you.

Love Always,
Tom

Receiving this passionately tender message propelled me back into my own heart and deepened my connection with not only my own soul, but with Tom's as well. It cleared away the blockage I had previously felt and inspired me to earnestly finish this book. And why wouldn't it? Tom's passion sparked my own and was the necessary ingredient I needed to write honestly.

Clearing the passageway to your heart is essential for genuine intimacy. Perform a "vulnerability-scan," on a scale from 1-10, with "1" being low and "10" being high. How open is your heart? Be really honest. Uncovering your heart is the most important thing you will ever do. If you've been hurt in the past (and we all perceive we've been hurt to some degree), are you keeping your heart closed, perhaps even a portion of it? In relationship, do you tend to withdraw your love or "pull back" to protect yourself from the possibility of getting hurt?

I remember counseling a couple who consistently engaged in the all too common pattern of "attack/defend/withdraw." The woman felt her partner was not taking enough responsibility for issues within the relationship, and at the time, he wasn't. But through the process of healing, he began seeing the role he played and how he contributed to the issues they were experiencing. During one session, he was especially honest and vulnerable. Exposing his feelings, he shared from his heart and took responsibility. Yet to my surprise, the woman retreated and became silent. When I asked her why, she replied, "He never takes responsibility for what's going on. He always dumps his stuff on me." "But," I said, "he just did. He shared with you how he sees his role in the relationship." As I watched the dynamics unfold, I saw she was scared. Having become accustomed to him not taking responsibility, she was convinced the relationship was "over." Yet, his willingness to be accountable changed everything. Or, at least, it changed her excuse for walking away from it.

Looking into her eyes, I gently asked, "Right now, I sense you have put up a thick wall between the two of you. Are you willing to let it down?" Tearfully she looked at me and stated with heartfelt honesty, "I don't know. I feel that if I let it down I'll have to let a lot more painful stuff surface and it terrifies me." "But," I reminded her, "you and I both know the pain from shutting your heart down is much more painful than addressing your issues." "Yes, I know," she sighed. And with that sigh came the recognition that now was not the time to put on the brakes. Now was the time for her to move forward with courage realizing her Higher Self was by her side and that she was safe in surrendering to the power of love.

This woman knew her relationship was over if she allowed her wall to remain in place, yet the relationship had tremendous capacity for healing and joy if she faced her fears. This experience reminds me of the passionate lyrics in the song "The Power of Love" performed by Celine Dion:

> *We're heading for something, somewhere*
> *I've never been,*
> *Sometimes I am frightened,*
> *But I am ready to learn of the power of love…*

All of us are afraid of love. *A Course in Miracles* teaches us that it is our *light*, not our darkness that frightens us. And what we fear most is love. It's no wonder we create countless blocks to intimacy in our relationships, not to mention the barriers to love we build around our own heart. I know people who hinder intimacy in myriad ways, including engaging in various tasks while talking on the phone, eating while cleaning or reading— anything to avoid being in the moment.

Yet it's the attempt to "protect" ourselves that causes us pain. In my own life, I have suffered the most when I've withdrawn my love, shielded my heart and/or avoided love—all motivated from the insane belief that if I don't, I will get hurt.

Ask yourself, "When am I most tempted to 'protect' myself? Do I believe I must guard my heart in order to remain unharmed? Am I allowing past wounds to affect present openness and intimacy? Is it common for me to avoid situations I perceive may hurt me, even though I care deeply? Am I allowing fear of rejection to keep me from pursuing loving and open connections? How willingly do I sit with my feelings and allow myself to feel them?" Answering these questions as honestly as possible builds a gateway for your heart to open and your relationships to flourish.

Intimacy cannot flow freely when we turn off the faucet of loving energy. We control the stream of intimacy by being open to giving and receiving love. Remind yourself that you do not deserve to go through life having dry, barren relationships. You deserve to experience genuine honesty, true intimacy and heartfelt passion. God desires for you to be happy, and relationships are a sacred temple in which to share His Infinite Love.

Starting right now, be willing to feel the power of love inside of you. Dare to go beyond your fear and embrace the love available to you with all of your heart and soul. The power of love is staggering; it has the ability to heal addictions, cure disease, and transform past pain into present happiness. Love is the glue that holds our universe together and is the reason we exist. Never underestimate its potency or presence. It's inside of you, it's inside of me, it's everywhere.

PRAYER FOR DEEPENED INTIMACY WITH OTHERS...

"Dear Mother/Father God, I ask for Your divine guidance and strength in lifting the veils of denial that are keeping me from recognizing and healing my issues, so I may gracefully mature into the loving man/woman You created me to be. I am willing to see and honor the light inside myself and to release any self-imposed limitations that are blocking the truth of who I am. Through Your love, I embrace my own wholeness, and accept that I, and others are already complete and loving beings. I accept that I have the inner-strength to speak my truth with loving intention so that my words and actions may help heal my relationships, and, the world. And so it is...Amen."

SEXUAL INTIMACY

"...sexual intimacy means...that to welcome yourself into your own heart as your guest, you now welcome your partner with the same acceptance and love."

Margot Anand, *The Art of Sexual Ecstasy*

THE MARRIAGE OF SEXUALITY AND SPIRITUALITY

*F*or years, I struggled with how to integrate my sexuality into my spiritual growth. Realizing that I am a "spiritual being having a human experience" and that our bodies are "a means of communication" has often left me feeling confused as to how my sexuality, the physical and energetic aspect of me, fits with my spirituality—the God-created, non-physical aspect of me. Always an avid reader, I remember frequently asking myself, "Why is there not more information on integrating our sexuality into our spirituality? Except for a few authors specializing in Tantric Sex, I have not found this sensitive issue thoroughly addressed from a spiritual standpoint. Therefore, since my soul has led me on a journey of intimacy, I will share what I have learned from my own life and how spirituality and sexuality can wed in a healthy and enjoyable manner.

We are faced with many paradoxes on the spiritual path: we are both spirit and matter, infinite and finite, immortal and mortal. Our greatest challenge is to embrace both our humanness and divinity and accept that they co-exist. We do not have to disregard one for the other, nor should we if we desire genuine self-love. Many of us believe if we are truly "spiritual," we will not have strong sexual appetites, nor will we look sexy or allow our sexual energy to be expressed in a way that anyone would notice. In fact, the temptation for many is to use spirituality as a means for repressing our sexuality. The guilt around our bodies and sexual behavior has been exacerbated by organized religion. We often unconsciously fear that God is watching over our genitals and judging us based on our sexual behavior.

In our society, it seems around thirteen years old we somehow lose our innocence. Because our breasts are sprouting or hormones are raging, we now have the potential to be "naughty" or "bad" in ways we could not possibly have been before. Look back at your life and notice the time in your development when you began to feel less pure, bad or naughty.

As a society, we are extremely confused about healthy sexual relations. Men have been taught to equate sex with love and affection, and women have learned to manipulate men through sex. Just look at the numerous shows and movies that flaunt sexual manipulation and seductive power, and you will see that most of our programming on sex and our own sexuality is very sick indeed.

When I was younger, a female relative once handed me the book *The Total Woman* and told me to read it because it would help me to learn how to "satisfy a man." I remember skimming through some of the pages and thinking, "What garbage!" Satisfying a man meant wearing something sexy, playing dumb and compromising myself merely to inflate his ego. Even at that naive age, I knew that was not the way to a man's heart and soul, at least, not any man *I* wanted.

A man I was once involved told me that men desire relationship with women because women have the innate ability of connecting them to their soul. This made sense to me because I've noticed that women who access their own desire and inner strength and are true to themselves have the ability to inspire others—male and female—to connect with their souls. And likewise, men who have the guts to open their heart and feel what they feel have the capacity to empower others—female and male—to heal and love unconditionally.

Our sexuality can be a powerful pathway to healing, so let's begin by taking a "sexual and spiritual inventory." Start with your thoughts and feelings: What is your perception of sex? How do you feel about your sexuality? Do you believe it's spiritual to be sexual? Do you think your sexuality and spirituality can co-exist in a healthy manner? What were your parent's beliefs about sex? What kind of sexual relations did they have?

Many people · believe they are unable to answer this last question because they never saw their parents being affectionate, or taking the time to have sex. Yet if you are really willing to look at the dynamics being played out between your parents (or whoever raised you), you will recall patterns of behavior that were exhibited and comments that were made about sex. All of these memories help you to more deeply understand your own perceptions about sex and your own sexuality.

Once while teaching an empowering workshop on spiritual growth, a lively discussion on what it means to be "spiritual" ensued. Participants raised their hands and shared their perceptions. A list was quickly created that revealed "what is *not* spiritual." It became clear that most did not believe it is "spiritual" to be 1) wealthy, 2) sexy, and/or 3) famous. As the conversation developed, it also became clear that it's not surprising so many on the spiritual path are struggling with abundance and sexual intimacy!

After having created the list of "what is not spiritual," our group was left with someone who lives a very sterile, dispassionate and probably boring life. Yuck! I don't know about you, but the thought of continuing on my spiritual pilgrimage would be very soul-less and unappealing if it meant I had to give up the desire for being passionate, abundant and filled with aliveness.

Projection makes perception, which simply means your beliefs about spirituality and sexuality influence every area of your life, particularly your ability to be intimate with yourself and others. For example, if you've been taught that it is not "spiritual" to be sexual, or that a truly "spiritual person" is someone who is not concerned with being sexually intimate, then voilá, your experiences will mirror that back to you. If you believe that spiritual people should not be sexy, or the other way around, that sexy people are not truly spiritual, your tendency will be to repress your own sexuality and passion while judging others who are embracing theirs.

This example always makes me think of Madonna. I believe Madonna represents someone who has come full circle with both her sexuality and spirituality. In fact, it appears her sexuality has been a pathway to her spiritual growth. Madonna is a wonderful role model for she demonstrates that one can be bold, beautiful, sexy, wealthy *and* spiritual. No wonder she pushes so many buttons!

As spiritual pioneers, it's important to embrace our humanness, including our sexuality. In fact, the appreciation of our physical body and its desires is a pathway to healing. So many of us on the spiritual path are tempted to eschew our bodies and emotions, convinced that it's not "spiritual" to feel sexual or get angry, when, actually, squelching these feelings leads us further into fear and away from our inner light. We must experience the pain before we can release it. This is the same thing as saying we must go through the darkness to get to the light. There is no short cut or easy way out. Each of us will need to travel through the cave of our subconscious and heal our perceptions before we will emerge into the light of higher awareness.

Some additional questions to consider are, "Am I sexually fulfilled? Am I comfortable expressing myself through the act of lovemaking? Do I feel safe being both vulnerable and sexual with my partner? Are there areas of my sexuality that are in need of awakening and/or healing?" If you have felt hurt or violated either physically, sexually or emotionally, forgiveness and the releasing of anger and shame must occur in order for you to feel okay about your body and sexuality. Healing these issues leads to feeling safe, and a safe context is imperative for intimacy to occur.

There have been countless times in my life that I have cried after having an orgasm for no apparent reason. For years, I never understood this reaction and it remained a curious phenomenon to me. Why, after such pleasure, would I cry? Sometimes it seemed to be from joy, but often, an unknown and ancient pain would surface. I have since come to realize that it doesn't matter *why* I cry as much as that I give myself permission to express myself. Of course, I can only do so when feeling safe and loved by my partner. A supportive and loving context is essential to exposing my feelings in such an ardent way. But the point is, allowing myself to be so unabashedly vulnerable stems from the intimacy I experience within myself, and crying from this soulful place enables me to genuinely and deeply unite with my own soul as well as the soul making love with me.

Healing our perceptions of our sexuality is just as important as healing our relationships, finances, physical bodies, etc. In fact, it's critical to experiencing genuine intimacy. Sexual healing occurs as you accept yourself, just as you are. It involves recognizing your desires, fears, sexual preference and letting go of any attachment to what others deem important. Further, believing "sex is dirty" is the same as believing "sex is everything." There is no difference. Both perceptions are false and must be healed.

Spiritual awakening requires letting go of judgment, yet we often become more judgmental on the spiritual path before we choose to let it go. That's why it is so helpful to be honest about our perceptions. We are only healed through conscious awareness. Thus if you are judging what "spiritual" and "sexual intimacy" look like, you will be judging *yourself* and holding yourself back from becoming the magnificent creation you were born to be.

It's important we remember our true essence is spirit—pure love and light. And nothing can alter that truth, not sexual addiction or sexual repression. To deny our physical reality is not the pathway to God. To accept and honor our physical reality and all of its experiences *is.*

Be willing to heal your sexuality by becoming aware of the judgment you are holding about yourself and others and be willing to let it go. Right now, dare to accept yourself! This includes letting go of judgment towards your thoughts, feelings, fears and desires. When you are tempted to judge yourself, for anything, ask yourself, "Could I really change or mar what God created just by my thinking, feeling, doing _____?" And the gentle but firm answer you will hear beneath the ego's critical insistence will be, "No." Spirit, recognizing you as Itself, sees only love, light and greatness. And so it is.

THE SENSUOUS SOUL

Just as sexual energy has helped man out of his spiritual state into the body, so it can help him to return in full awareness to his divine primal state of wholeness.

Elizabeth Haich, *Sexual Energy and Yoga*

Our desire for intimacy, like the current along the ocean floor, runs very, very deep. Sexual intimacy involves the intensity of our emotions as well as the aliveness of our spiritual selves, for it encompasses the arousal of our body, mind and spirit. It is a heightened state of awareness, that when reached, creates an aura of excitement and passion that can be soulfully expressed through the physical realm. During sexual intimacy, we are literally *making love*; we're expressing love from the depths of who we are and physically sharing this truth with another.

Our yearning to connect with another is so compelling because it enables us to connect with the God-energy in the other and us. It's akin to tasting God, feeling God, and knowing God. Since God resides within us, it's as though we are bridging the separation we feel from God while existing in this third dimensional reality. And we do so by becoming emotionally naked. As we strip away the layers of fear that clothe our body and soul, we can say with raw passion: "I desire to connect all of me with all of you." Emotional, heartfelt honesty—with ourselves and others—leads to sexual intimacy.

I don't profess to be a sexual expert, but my experiences have taught me that the art of sexual intimacy and ecstasy provides us the opportunity to share ourselves, express our love, and look beyond the appearance of another into the depth of their soul. It can involve a loving experience, erotic experience, soulful experience, or all three. It allows us to channel our creative energy in a sexual manner, just as our creativity can be an outlet for expressing our sexual energy. Sexual intimacy differs from merely having sex because it involves the soul. Sex without soul is like food without flavor; you may eat it but that doesn't necessarily mean you will fully taste it or savor its richness. So many of us settle for having routine or soul-less sex because that's all we know. Countless women have been taught to satisfy a man's need for love through sex, and numerous men have been programmed to believe that having sex with a woman equates to love. Yet sexual intimacy goes so much deeper than merely being sexual.

When I was younger, I used to think much of my worth stemmed from sexually pleasing others. At an early age I bought into society's belief that a woman's seduction is her key to power and acceptance (as consistently portrayed through television, movies and magazines). Thus, the more I was considered "good in bed," the more fragile my ego's shaky self-esteem became. It wasn't until years later that I realized basing my self-worth on sex was the demise of my sense of self. Of course, whenever we value ourselves for something other than who we are (love), we're going to suffer. And suffer I did. For on a deeper level, I knew I was not being cared about for who I was, but for what I did. I learned I would never experience genuine love through my sexual behavior for I wasn't loving and honoring myself; I was only compromising who I was out of fear and low self-worth. Years later after much emotional and spiritual growth, I discovered that I needed to do nothing to be more lovable than I already was. This awareness led to stronger boundaries and the ability to say "*No*" when a loving and intimate connection was missing.

Sexual intimacy, like any other form of intimacy, involves the willingness to give, receive, expand and embrace. Therefore, as previously discussed, it's imperative we understand that each of us has both a female and male aspect. Our feminine aspect is *receptive*, providing us with the desire and ability to be nurturing, sensitive and empathetic, while our masculine aspect is *active*, giving us the strength to be discerning, assertive and productive. Both are equally important, for on a higher level, the feminine is how we experience the word of God while the masculine is how we express God's message into our relationships.

Sexually, we possess both aspects, and personally, I believe we are androgynous at our core. When we attain balance between our feminine and masculine aspects, we unite our inner-female's sensitivity and vulnerability with our inner-male's passion and desire. However, when we are out of balance, we may feel shut down and repressed or sexually needy and demanding. So, identifying our sexual behaviors can be a pathway to healing not only our sexuality, but our relationships as well.

Understanding and accepting your sexuality is critical to experiencing heightened emotional and sexual intimacy, as well as healthy self-esteem. For how can you possibly feel comfortable being intimate if you are not comfortable with your own sexuality? As both spiritual and sexual beings, our sexuality may be seen as existing somewhere along a "continuum" ranging from heterosexuality to homosexuality. For example, "The Kinsey Heterosexual-Homosexual Scale" helps people understand that our sexuality is not static but fluid and dwells anywhere from "exclusively heterosexual" to "exclusively homosexual."

However, living in our narrow thinking world, our egos feel a need to label everything, including our sexuality. And for most people, labels that do not fit into the "heterosexual box" trigger anxiety, guilt and fear. Whenever I work with people in healing their sexuality, I first ask them to let go of their attachment to labels. Perhaps they have sexual preferences that have been repressed simply because of the homophobic society we reside in. For example, through my work, I am finding that countless women are feeling more emotionally connected to their female friends than to their spouses. Louise Hay points out in her book *Empowering Women,* the trend reveals that many women are feeling comfortable bonding intimately with other women on the path of personal growth, and that gay relationships are on the rise: "Today we are finding that many older women, who would never have thought of doing so in the past, are now beginning to explore a gay lifestyle and turning to other women for intimate relationships...Intimacy with another woman can reveal depths that women have never experienced before."

Coming to terms with your sexuality is a critical step in increasing your personal intimacy and relations with others. It's also important to remember that your sexual desires and preferences can change. Nothing is ever in stone; as souls in process, we are always changing and that means our sexuality can change, too!

If we are to accept our sexuality, it's important that we learn to let go of the guilt we have about our bodies. Because of traditional religious conditioning, there is a tremendous amount of guilt around both sex and the body, making it difficult to achieve and sustain intimacy. I have yet to meet a person who does not possess some guilt around his or her body and sexual behavior.

The amount of sexual violations and molesting occurring within our families is staggering and indicative of the amount of sexual guilt and repression we carry. If you have been sexually violated, it's important you seek assistance in releasing any shame or guilt. It's virtually impossible to have healthy boundaries or relations until the guilt and shame are released and transmuted. I have found that the individuals who are willing to do the inner work it requires to deal with such wounds are also the people who learn to fuel their energies into healing and creative endeavors. When channeled appropriately, strong sexual energy, or energy that has been repressed, can be a powerful pathway to spiritual and creative ascension.

God longs for us to be happy and our sexual desire is meant to bring us joy. Joy occurs as we invite God into our sexual experiences. Yet, because we have such guilt around our bodies and sexuality, we often feel we must "split" ourselves and separate our sexual passion from our daily life. In fact, sometimes our love for our partner when combined with day-to-day living can actually evaporate our sexual desire. It's not that we don't love him or her, but we don't know how to balance being responsible, loving, and supportive with being passionate, erotic, and spontaneous. For many, it feels imperative that our "wantonness" be kept apart from our role of partner, mother, father, daughter, son, or friend. I remember a man once sharing his frustration about his spouse, who at the time was a fairly new mother. He openly declared, "I want my wife back!" and it was clear that though he respected her maternal role, he very much missed the passion they had shared prior to their children's presence.

Sexual energy is a potent and creative power, meant to expand the light and love in each of us. When we align ourselves with God, we open the doors to all of our chakras which allows us to experience ecstasy for hours. Yet we must be willing to release the guilt we carry from believing that sex is somehow "bad" or "dirty." Sex can be a pathway to deepened intimacy and heightened joy.

Learn to be present in your body. Once while driving with a friend, we were reading a passage from a book that discussed experiencing the power of God through one's sexuality. At the same time, Sophie B. Hawkins was singing on the radio. (If you are unfamiliar with Sophie, she is a very passionate, uninhibited and sensual artist). My friend exclaimed, "I'm having a hard time reading about God joining in my lovemaking while listening to Sophie!" I replied, "But that's exactly what the book is saying. We need to unite the spiritual with the sexual. Why *can't* God be a part of the sexual act? God could if we would let go of the false and inhibiting perception that God is an old man in the clouds looking down at our nakedness and judging us!"

The book *Angel Blessings* affirms, "Sexual energy and spiritual energy come from the same source. The creative power of sexuality ignites the fire of passion to fill your body with aliveness. The joy and vitality that accompany this energy connect you with your Eternal Self. Invite Anael [angel of sexuality] to guide you on this path of exploration until passion becomes a powerful, spiritual link combining love for yourself and love for your partner with love for God."

I remember another time when I was discussing kundalini energy with a friend. As the conversation progressed she posed the question, "Do you feel that you are in your body most of the time?" My initial thought was, "Of course I'm in my body, where *else* would I be?" But instead of responding, I allowed myself to sit with this question. As time passed, I began to realize I was living much of my life not in my body, but in my head.

Jungian analyst and author Marion Woodman shares a poignant story on her tape series *Sitting by the Well* that illustrates this point. While visiting India she had an out-of-body experience and discovered she desired to be *spirit* not *matter*. In other words, she was more comfortable living in the spiritual and intellectual realm than in her physical suit of flesh and blood, complete with its desires, reactions and instinctual energy. Upon this realization she began connecting more deeply with her body and using it and her dreams as a means for understanding the realm of the unconscious. This approach became a catalyst for transformation for both herself and others. Marion believes the body is an instrument of truth; it reveals all of the fears, conflicts and emotions we've repressed and have housed within our physical dwelling.

Being in the moment with our bodies keeps us grounded in the present moment. How many times have you started having sex with your partner only to discover your mind is wandering to some other place and time? It's impossible to surrender and become stimulated when you are not fully present. Getting out of your head and into your body opens the door and allows sexual energy to flow through. Putting your body in bed is not enough. Your thoughts, feelings and attention must be there, too. The goal is to have energy flowing between body, spirit *and* mind.

One way to practice becoming more present in your body is to begin noticing when your thoughts are allowing you to drift out of the moment. For example, I've observed my mind wandering to past or future events while walking outside, sometimes to the extent that I've missed the beauty of nature around me! Noticing this habit was my first step in correcting it. Next, I began practicing refocusing my thoughts to what was around me in that particular moment. Being sexual with someone is no different. You must be willing to let go of thoughts and concerns that distract you from the experience. Focusing on your breathing is a good place to start. Deep breathing will allow you to receive pleasure from your partner while moving your energy from your head down into your heart and lower body.

Sexual energy has the power to balance your chakras and promote healing within your psyche and body. Becoming comfortable with verbally expressing yourself during lovemaking is another powerful tool for enhanced pleasure, intimacy and healing. Our root chakra expands as we allow our feelings of stimulation to move up through our body and into our throat. It not only increases our pleasure while in bed; it helps clear the throat chakra so we may comfortably speak our truth when *out* of bed. Songwriter and singer, Tori Amos, is a good example of this. She so arduously and erotically expresses her sexual energy while singing that just listening to her stirs the energy in one's own throat and soul. Tori also uses her lyrics to help rape survivors heal the emotional wounds that occur from sexual violations. Her music has been a pathway to healing for many and her lyrics have empowered countless women to seek sexual healing.

Appreciate your body. A challenging task for most, practicing appreciation and gratitude of our bodies is a powerful avenue to remaining centered and present. Many of us have very poor perceptions of our bodies and the negative self-talk we engage in only diminishes our desire. If you are a woman whose mother is (or was) critical of her own body, you must be willing to re-program your belief about your body. The "negative mother" that resides within us is critical, controlling and manipulating, and listening to her internal voice will invalidate even your best intentions toward enjoying your body.

While growing up, I never heard my mother criticize *my* body, but I did hear her invalidate her *own* body, which produced the same effect. It took me years to recognize the amount of destructive faultfinding I was engaging in with my own body. After repeatedly hearing me complain about flaws only visible to my critical eyes, my husband, (after years of complimenting me) ran out of patience and exclaimed, "Enough is enough! You have a beautiful body, would you just learn to accept that?!?" Hearing the exasperation in his voice motivated me to look at why I was being so hard on myself. It dawned on me that I was unconsciously expressing my mother's disdain for her own body, and it was time for me to heal this harmful programming.

If this resonates to you, keep in mind that we are always healed through conscious awareness. Bringing any self-defeating aspect into your consciousness is the first step toward releasing it and replacing it with loving self-acceptance. Practice affirming this truth: "My body is a miraculous, sensual vehicle designed for me to lovingly express my deepest self."

Embrace your sexuality and release attachment to others' opinions. We've discussed the importance of coming to terms with your sexuality, but letting go of your attachment to what others think of you is just as critical in being true to yourself. If you truly want personal freedom and lasting happiness, you must be willing to live your life in a way that nourishes your soul and feeds your spirit. You cannot afford to live according to the expectations of others. This includes the "voices" in your head that sound like "mother" and "father." So many of us identify with what we've been taught that it's no joke we not only take ourselves into bed, but the sexual perceptions of our mothers and fathers, too! Until we learn to separate what is true for us versus what others want, we will allow our past conditioning and present friends and family to dictate how we are going to live.

What are *your* desires? What is in *your* heart? Explore your sexual fantasies and uncover what your heart yearns for. Be daring, be bold and clear the inhibiting baggage that binds your sexual flow.

Keep in mind that your life is all you control because it's just that, *your* life. If you choose not to decide how you want to live your life, there are countless others who will. Society will gladly dictate what your sexuality should be and what your relationships should look like. Zig Ziglar once declared, "If you do not live the life you believe, you will believe the life you live." Take your power back by becoming aware of *your truth*. Then, dare to live it. An authentic life is a powerful life; nothing is more charismatic than the person who is real and unafraid to live life according to his or her own truth, not someone else's.

PRAYER FOR HEALING SEXUAL INTIMACY...

"Dear Mother/Father God, help me heal the thoughts, fears and behaviors I possess that are barriers to intimacy and the presence of Love's awareness. In this moment, I am willing to release any self-imposed thoughts that inhibit my ability to experience healthy, loving sexual relations. I desire to let go of the judgment I carry about my sexuality as well as the perceptions I carry toward people whose sexual orientation differs from mine. I am ready to release the guilt I carry from my past sexual experiences. Right now, I honor myself as a loving and lovable spiritually sexual being. I pay tribute to my body and the passion *and love it yearns to express. I recognize God desires for me to experience my humanness in all its glory and that my sexuality is a beautiful part of who I am. And so it is...Amen."*

BRINGING IT ALL HOME: LIVING THE INTIMATE LIFE...

It's a funny thing about life; if you refuse to accept anything but the best, you very often get it.

Somerset Maugham

*Y*ou are meant to live an intimate and authentic life, a life that honors the depth of who you are, a life that nourishes your heart and expands your mind, a life that is unencumbered with what others think, a life that empowers you to be who you really are.

And yet, the question may remain, "How can I live such a life on a day-by-day, hour-by-hour and moment-by-moment basis?" "What steps can I take, today, toward heartfelt intimacy?" In my own life, and in the work that I perform with others, I have found the following practices to be invaluable and successful components in experiencing genuine intimacy with your deepest self, God, and others:

Give with "heart-centered" meaning:

Giving to "get" anything makes it impossible to create a safe space and thus is the death of intimacy. Conditions and demands will literally "dry up" your intimate juices. *Love without limits entails keeping your love pure.* If you desire to do something for someone merely to have your needs met, or to fill some void, intimate contact between the two of you will become forced, routine, or non-existent and the relationship will eventually breakdown.

For example, I believe our sexual, creative and spiritual energy stem from the same source. When I feel inspired to write a book or create a new workshop, I often feel the need to conserve my energy and direct it toward creating. Sometimes it appears to my partner that I am not as "available" as much as other times. The absolute worst thing he could do is put pressure on me, either overtly or covertly. By not honoring my need for "space" he pushes me away which is exactly what he *doesn't* want. Keeping this in mind, if I sense my partner's feelings are hurt or that he is feeling rejected by me, we discuss what it is he *really* wants which helps him access the deeper part of himself and dissolve any "neediness" he may be feeling.

<u>Look inward for your fulfillment, not outward:</u>

Within you resides a deep well of creativity, love and inner "gifts." When you are willing to access your inherent strength and fulfill the purpose you were born to accomplish, you cannot help but feel complete and whole. Loving what we do and doing what we love prevent us from feeling deprived, for how can we possibly feel empty when we're fulfilling our divine purpose?

Unfortunately, for various reasons, many of us are not in touch with our inherent gifts. One of the biggest reasons is that discovering our inner talents means we are then responsible for using them. Once we know our life's purpose, we must follow it or in many ways, it can feel like the death of our soul. Also, following our heart frequently requires making some changes in our life. Yet our ego abhors change and will do most anything to keep us stuck in a predictable rut. Stretching beyond our comfort zone and taking leaps of faith are an integral part of fulfilling our purpose.

Further, relationships often suffer when we are afraid to delve into our spiritual creativity, which can take innumerable forms. Fear of failure or success, letting go of attachments to people's opinions, releasing the familiar, and so on can keep us stuck. When this happens, we often turn to our partner to fulfill us, which then drains the energy from the relationship. No wonder we're left feeling so needy! Yet when we give to others and extend from our soul, we're able to join with another at the end of the day feeling rejuvenated and overflowing with an abundance of loving energy. This serves to revitalize and nurture the relationship.

Turn within to become aware of what is driving your needs. Is it because you are feeling unloved, scared or lonely? Practice giving what you want to receive. We all want to feel loved for who we are, not for what we do. If you are feeling empty, look within and ask for guidance from your higher self: "Help me to recognize the abundance of love and light I have within me so I may express it to those I love." Extending love is the fastest way to fill any emptiness you feel.

Appreciate the love you receive, including genuine displays of affection from another:

Accepting love and affection from others builds abundance and gratitude over time. It helps us see the glass, or relationship, half full rather than half empty. How many times have you complained about the lack of attention or nurturing you've received only to find out that your partner feels they are giving a lot? So often, it's our perception that needs changing, not the amount of activity. Further, the more you appreciate, the more you're going to receive—that's just the way it works!

A powerful tool for practicing loving appreciation is to keep a daily "love log." At the end of each day, jot down the times throughout the day that you chose to give and receive love—all of them. It doesn't matter if it involved extending love to your pet or the teller at the bank. Doing this will keep you in a loving state of mind and enhance your ability to experience genuine love while affirming your truth as a light-filled child of God.

Let go of guilt!:

All of us carry guilt deep within our minds. You may ask, "Guilt over what?" And the answer is, not only do we have guilt for feeling separated from our Creator, but we retain guilt for all of the mistakes we've ever made. No one is harder on us than we are on ourselves, *no one*. And yet, *A Course in Miracles* reminds us that "mistakes are not sins." We only waste precious life force when we beat ourselves up for past thoughts and behaviors. Instead, we could just as easily forgive ourselves for mistakes we have made if we choose.

This reminds me of a time in my life when I had worked very hard at letting go of a destructive pattern. I felt that I had broken the pattern and for quite some time, I felt emotionally free. I was grateful to have released a trait that had influenced my life for many years. Then one evening, the same behavior re-surfaced. I was both dismayed and guilt-ridden. The next day, I was tempted to criticize myself, but soon after, I realized that wallowing in remorse was exactly what my ego wanted me to do. Recognizing the ego's addiction to pain, I chose instead, to learn from the situation and *let the rest go!* I could feel the temptation to feel bad about myself, yet a stronger inner presence invited me to laugh at the notion that anything I did could make me "bad" or somehow tarnish my true essence. That particular event was an invaluable lesson for me, and my day, week and *life* improved dramatically upon that realization.

Address issues within your relationships:

Nothing will squelch your intimacy and passion faster than unresolved issues in your relationship, *nothing*. When we feel angry or hurt toward someone we care about, it is very difficult to connect emotionally. Repressed anger is like a vice that wraps itself around the relationship and squeezes the life force from it. Whenever I hear couples sharing their lack of sexual passion or emotional intimacy, I know there is anger lurking somewhere beneath the surface and that healing is needed. Looking at, and resolving issues, builds an invaluable and mighty bridge to intimacy. It demonstrates your love for your partner as well as your love for yourself.

Further, it provides an opportunity for sharing and healing which are major factors in deepening intimacy. I often hear how one partner (usually, but not always, the male or masculine partner) is not interested in talking about issues. In fact, it's not uncommon for one partner to think that everything is just "fine" when in reality, the other feels misunderstood and invalidated for his or her feelings. Since this is a frequent concern in my counseling sessions and workshops, my first response is, "Are you letting your partner know that it's important to you to address issues?" Too often, we expect the other person to *know* what we want which is unfair and unrealistic. Also, "Are you speaking your truth and allowing your partner to do so without judgment?" Learning to speak our truth with pure intention is essential to healing a relationship and increasing intimacy. If we truly desire genuineness in our relationships, we must be willing to lift the veils of denial and address the issues that hang between us.

I remember counseling a couple who complained of a lack of passion in their relationship. As they continued talking, they revealed there was very little discussion taking place between them and that they considered the other to be "indifferent." With some probing it became clear there were layers of anger that had never been discussed. Their approach involved sweeping issues under the rug for they were not sure how to share from the heart or speak their truth without blaming the other.

Through relationship counseling, they learned to cultivate a safe, non-blaming space in which to share. The walls that had kept them from enjoying genuine intimacy began to disintegrate as they became empowered to speak from their deeper selves without becoming defensive. In fact, they found that the anger they felt toward each other went deeper, much deeper. They became aware that they were in need of healing wounds that proceeded the relationship, hurts and "shadow beliefs" that stemmed from childhood. It led them to appreciating themselves and each other in a newfound way, and they are now a wonderful role model for other couples.

Denying and avoiding issues creates invisible walls that become thicker and thicker with each unresolved concern. They isolate us from our selves and the other person and lead to a breakdown of truth, intimacy and integrity. Creating an empowering context in which to address issues requires developing a "safe" environment for your partner to share his or her truth. This means letting go of judgment and listening with an exposed heart and open mind.

There was a time in my life when I avoided speaking my truth. Feeling unsafe sharing myself from fear of being judged and rejected, I would conceal what I really felt. But through the journey of spiritual growth, my husband and I made healing and intimacy our priority and agreed we would not judge what was being shared. As this occurred, I began feeling safe enough to express what I felt. Our dedication to providing support and love without conditions helped both of us build a safe haven in which to share.

Honor each other by addressing issues. Like weeds in a beautiful garden, they must be tugged out and removed at their core so they don't grow back. Take a leap of faith by speaking your truth with love and conviction. Looking at issues, as scary as it may be, will lead to stronger love and an exquisite garden of intimacy.

Daily, purify your intentions:

Intention, like thoughts and feelings, is energy and is very, very powerful. Your intentions are the 'thought-seeds' you cast out into the universe each and every day, which literally—not metaphorically—create your landscape.

If your intention is to live a life that is real, congruent, healed and filled with integrity, then everything that is not authentically you will reveal itself so you can choose to strip it away. Yet if your intention is split between wanting one of the Three P's: Power/Prestige/Prosperity *and* wanting intimacy and joy, then you will experience the effects of your split-thinking and your life will never, ever, be completely fulfilling.

Practice purifying your intention. Something as common as your daily conversations provides you with an excellent opportunity for observing your intentions and infusing them with love and genuineness. Before you say something, begin noticing *why* you're about to say it. What is your intention? I've found this to be a very healing and empowering practice. I've also discovered how it can take a superficial conversation in which one or both parties are avoiding their truth to a deeper and more "real" place. For example, there have been times in my life when I have questioned the intention of what the other is saying and have asked, point blank, "What is your intention for saying that?" Nothing has shifted the dynamics of a conversation faster. Now keep in mind that it's important that you are clear as to *your* intention before posing that question!

A wonderful technique for clarifying and setting your own intention is to start each day by writing a paragraph or two about the qualities you would like to experience that day. First, take a few moments to reflect on how you'd like your day to go and what essences you'd like to capture. Then, put it on paper as a way of sending it out into the universe with love and light. Try it. You'll be amazed at how this simple practice works!

<u>Rely on higher guidance in all that you do:</u>

Quite honestly, if you followed only this suggestion, you're on your way home. For nothing has the capacity to provide more self-love, emotional freedom and lasting fulfillment than *asking* and *following* your Inner Guidance.

One of the intensive workshops I teach is titled The Self-Mastery Program. Often upon completion of the weekend retreat, I ask the participants to share their definition of "self-mastery." Most will agree they have learned that genuine "mastery of self" has nothing to do with mastering anything externally, with using the power of one's mind to "get" something, with doing anything which merely serves to inflate one's feeling of self-importance or with "making things happen." The majority of people recognize that the art of "self-mastery" has everything to do with relying on higher guidance, and that no situation, issue or problem is too big or too small for Spirit to handle.

We need only ask, and we will find that our relationships, finances, and work begin to heal, and that our lives become fine-tuned instruments in which God can move through so we may be of help to others.

How many times per day do you ask for help from a Power greater than you? And, how often do you follow it? The amount of inner peace and happiness you experience in your life is directly proportionate to the amount of energy you expend on following the Voice within.

Be willing, right now, to ask for guidance in healing your fears of intimacy. Ask for help in releasing beliefs, thoughts and behaviors that do not honor your true essence. Start with, "Who am I, really? For so long I've based my perception of myself on what others think that I've forgotten who I am. So, who am I, truly?" "What does my soul want to hear?" Next, "How can I best share my authentic self with others?" "What steps can I take to live the life of an intimate soul?" Finally, be willing to hear the gentle yet firm Voice. That wise and loving Inner Voice will direct you home where your soul and God resides. As Emmet Fox once eloquently wrote:

> *God is Infinite Life. God is Boundless Love. God is Infinite Intelligence. God is Unfathomable Wisdom. God is Unspeakable Beauty. God is the Unchanging Principle of Perfect Good. God is the Soul of man.*

Such is the life of the intimate soul....

ACKNOWLEDGMENTS

My heartfelt gratitude goes to many people. First and foremost, I want to express my appreciation to my husband and business partner, Tom. His loving support has empowered me to not only write this book, but to experience genuine intimacy in every part of my life. Because of our relationship, I have come to know my deepest self while learning how to love and be loved by another. What could possibly be more important than that?

I also want to thank the following people: My daughter, Alexis, for her infinite supply of unconditional love; Bev, for her friendship, loving support and endless list of inspirational quotes; Pat, for her wonderful editing ability and helpful feedback; the Hoffman Institute for the emotional freedom they have provided to me and continue to extend to others; *A Course in Miracles* for helping me heal my relationships and experience the true meaning of love. Further, I wish to express my gratitude to all of the spiritually healing publications that have supported me in my journey and shared my writings with countless others.

Last, but certainly not least, I am forever grateful to all of the people I have been fortunate enough to encounter in my workshops, presentations and spiritual counseling sessions. Their openness, honesty, and willingness to grow inspires the healing work I continue to be blessed with. Truly, everyone is a mirror and every situation is a learning experience. Thus, all of the people I work with are many of my greatest teachers.

Namaste

Information on Laura's Workshops

<u>The Self-Mastery Program</u>

A transforming, healing, and inspiring weekend retreat for providing spiritual awakening and lasting emotional freedom...

Life transforming...Unite with your essential self, follow your heart's destiny and integrate your deepest aspirations with consistent action by taking full responsibility for your life. Radically different from self-improvement approaches, Self-Mastery focuses on your innate self, enabling you to remember that your essential self is far greater than any of life's events. Emotional barriers will be released through self-explorations to awaken your true self. By releasing negative beliefs and behaviors, you will be propelled beyond the limitations you've formerly accepted and carried to new levels of expanded joy and deepened spiritual integrity. Your Self-Mastery experience will provide:

Spiritual Awakening ** Emotional Freedom ** Fulfilling Your Life's Purpose **

CULTIVATING the INTIMATE LIFE

If you desire to experience genuine, heartfelt intimacy in your life, then this soulful and healing workshop is for you. Laura's program is specially designed to assist you in cultivating a joyfully intimate and authentic relationship with yourself and others. Benefits include:

*Ability to speak your truth with loving intention;

*Deepened connection with your soul;

*Releasing fears and "vicious cycles" that inhibit your ability to remain open, exposed and vulnerable;

*Greater capacity for experiencing self-love;

*Enhanced fulfillment in relationship with your deepest self and others.

The Art of Compassionate Forgiveness

The Art of Compassionate Forgiveness is a healing and transforming workshop on forgiveness based on the principles in *A Course in Miracles*. This workshop is for those who desire to learn genuine forgiveness, experience inner peace, feel with an open heart, and capture the beauty of fulfilled love as we continue the journey inward to wholeness.

The only requirement for attending this workshop is the willingness to forgive and the desire for inner peace.

Laura's Newsletter

Matters of the Heart—a free quarterly newsletter that will keep you updated on Laura's workshops while inspiring and empowering you in every area of your life.

To receive *Matters of the Heart* please call: 888.PEACE93, e-mail: laurahyde@novagate.com, or visit our website: www.laurahyde.com